Protecting Emilie

L. Heim

Dedicated to
Victims of Parental Alienation

PREFACE

My story is a detailed account of parental alienation and how such abuse changed one child's life forever. As the former stepmother of one of the many victims, I saw firsthand the emotional and physical devastation it caused, and almost death. The family court judges in our case disregarded the evidence and enabled a biological mother for more than a decade to harm her daughter through deceit, manipulations, and physical pain. My story isn't uncommon. In the media are actors like Alec Baldwin, Kelly Rutherford, and Jason Patric, who have publicly shared their battles to not have their children alienated from them. Children need both parents equally unless of course one of the parents is a sex offender or otherwise legally or mentally incompetent.

When I met Patton Young, he was newly divorced, kind, compassionate, and as intelligent as any woman could hope for to complete her family. We were both single parents with daughters. My daughter, McKenna, was three and absent of a biological father who chose to never meet her and Patton's daughter, Emilie, was two years old.

Two years after Patton and I met, we married. It didn't take long before we discovered that our lives would be immersed in the convoluted quest for justice against my husband's deceitful, ex-wife Andrea who selfishly brainwashed and used Emilie as a pawn in every way she could against her father.

In my family's case, the drama and torment over the years led to arrests, false abuse allegations, suicide watches, a litany of mental health issues, and finally the demise of our marriage. It all could have been prevented by the family law judges who believed in and enabled the abusive mother. When justice finally prevailed, it was too late, the damage was done.

It is my hope that the details and red flags in my story will wake up and educate our legislature, parents, teachers, coaches, counselors, and anyone involved with children in custodial conflict.

Parental alienation is real and it *is* child abuse.

"I'll leave but I will see you proven unfit!" True to form, Andrea had to get the last words in. With Emilie at her side she grabbed her hand and turned one last time to me. "And Emilie doesn't love you; she loves me and hates you!" The look of despair on Emilie's little face is forever etched in my mind. That day was what you call a game-changer but this was no game. It was the only the beginning of what Andrea had in store.

I: Pass Go and Collect a Red Flag

In a desired neighborhood, my townhouse was priced right for a couple not wanting a yard or exterior maintenance. As a thirty-five year old single mother of my almost three-year old daughter, McKenna, I longed for the peace of a single family home with a yard.

It was the last day in August, 2002; a typical Florida day with stagnate air and cloudless blue skies. My computer was temporarily situated in my dining room where I sat down to review the ad I had placed in the newspaper and on-line, for the open house I was having the following day. I liked to see what other comparables were available but to my chagrin, another townhouse just a few doors down was also on the market!

With trepidation, I decided to visit the neighbor to see how my place my compared with theirs. Since I never left McKenna alone, she was by my side when I knocked on my neighbor's door. We were quickly greeted by a friendly gentleman who stood just over six-foot tall. He seemed to be around my age and he too had a little girl next to him. As the smiling little blonde girl clutched the man's leg I noticed she had the same soft blue eyes as her father did. She was McKenna's polar opposite as my daughter inherited my brown eyes and hair.

After I explained the reason for my visit, the man introduced himself as Patton, and his daughter as Emilie.

1

He then graciously welcomed us inside to have a look around. I felt my palms sweat and my cheeks flush with color as I somehow felt awkwardly nervous, as if I were on some kind of blind date. I don't typically walk into a strange man's home, especially with my young child but I felt comfortable after seeing him interact so impressively with his vivacious daughter.

As Patton toured me through the home, he explained to me that this was not *his* home; he was merely staying there until his divorce was final, a couple of months later. His friend, Tom, who was a realtor, had bought it as an investment property and while on the market, agreed to let Patton stay there free of charge.

Although this was much more information than what I anticipated to hear, I felt badly for him. Patton seemed like such a friendly guy and was so attentive to his daughter.

Back downstairs, our daughters were playing with one of Emilie's toys. I ushered McKenna to the cramped foyer. Emilie waddled behind her like she had found a new best friend. I offered to have Emilie come over and play with McKenna and some of her toys. Patton seemed apprehensive at first but then agreed, as long as I didn't mind him coming over as well since he didn't really know me and I hadn't mentioned if anyone else lived at my house. I think he was being cautious; a sign of a conscientious parent.

Patton was interested in watching a football game so I turned on the television. We sat on the sofa in my living room and talked while the girls played in front of us with various toys from McKenna's overflowing toy box. I really liked talking with my new friend. He seemed so genuine, witty and, smart.

Although Patton was handsome, resembling a younger version of the actor Ed Harris, he was captivating me from inside. He was so intelligent and had a terrific sense of humor.

I told Patton how I had been a single parent since McKenna's birth and that she had never met her biological father except for an hour when she was a week old. John had been a charming boyfriend but not someone with whom I wanted to grow old. I had broken off our obligatory engagement during the first trimester of my pregnancy. I knew I made the right choice when he abstained from any kind of relationship with our daughter after meeting his newborn just once.

It made me sad for McKenna but I had actually come to appreciate having her all to myself every hour of every day. She was the sweetest, smartest, and most creative little girl I could have ever been blessed with!

When Patton and Emilie left an hour or so later, I smiled behind the closed door wondering if he might have any interest in someone like me: a single mother with three years of college but no Bachelor's degree and a new job as a full-time inside sale representative for a health insurance administrator. I was a little excited at the prospect of our friendship growing but quickly came back down to earth when I looked at my little McKenna, my "beauty," as I called her. She was so sweet, so innocent, so loving and so wonderful, I wasn't sure I would want to share my time with anyone but her.

The next morning, mid-way through my Open House, I was opening the door to let a prospective buying couple out when I saw Patton about to ring my doorbell. He quietly, but confidently, whispered "Here is my phone number. If you can get a sitter, I would love to take you out to dinner tonight. Emilie will be at her mother's." He handed me a crumply Post-It note and walked away allowing me to say good-bye to my visitors.

The house was now empty except for McKenna and me. I could feel my cheeks blushing as I thought about how long it had been. McKenna was almost three and counting my nine months of pregnancy, it had been nearly four years since I had any kind of date. I was flattered and excited. He was engaging, well spoken, was almost

3

legally divorced, and he knew what it was like to have a young child. He could be a terrific match, I thought.

I called Patton a bit later to offer an alternative since my mom was unable to watch McKenna. I asked if he would instead like to come over for a glass of wine after I put McKenna to sleep. I added that we could play some backgammon or watch a movie if he'd like. He agreed.

When Patton arrived, his cologne took my breath away; it had been too long since my senses were that aroused. As he walked across the threshold, his light blue eyes seemed to sparkle against his chiseled face covered with just a healthy hint of golfer's tan. I offered him a glass of wine and although I rarely, if ever drank alcohol, I joined him. I needed to loosen up and not be so nervous. We talked a lot over multiple games of backgammon. As the wine started to break down our barriers, we made a bet. Whoever won the next game would get a shoulder massage. I was starting to like this guy.

I enjoyed listening to his educated southern drawl define his past and present. He told me how he graduated from University of Florida and was a proud Gator. After law school at Stetson, he became a personal injury attorney and now had his own small firm in Tampa. He spoke about his soon-to-be ex-wife, Andrea, and how she had basically given him an ultimatum to get married. His friends were getting married and Andrea was insecure with their relationship.   He described her as quite the victim. He said she had used her victimization to gain pity or justify her mistakes and moods. Patton and Andrea eloped after only six months of dating despite his family and friends discouraging their union.

Less than a month after they got married, Andrea socked him in the face with the hand donning the protruding setting of her wedding ring causing a fat, bloodied lip. For him, it was the beginning of the end. The marriage was not stable, ever.   Andrea would apologize, manipulate, and reel him in before becoming violent again. It was a vicious cycle from which he needed to escape.

About here in the conversation, an abrupt banging on my front door jolted us both the way it would if we had been watching a horror movie. I ran to the kitchen and peeked out the window where my porch light shone on a pale, thin woman with large protruding breasts plunging from the neckline of her baby-blue tee shirt. She was wearing short-shorts and her hair was box-colored brassy with yellowish tints. I had no clue who she was or why she would be banging so persistently at my door at such a late hour, close to 11pm. Thinking she must have the wrong house, I spoke to her through the window.

"Hello, may I help you?" I asked.

She glared at me with squinted eyes and shouted crossly. "I need to see my husband and I know he is in there!"

Confused and shocked, I went into the living room to ask Patton. "Some woman is at the door asking for her 'husband!'" Although he seemed surprised, he composedly arose.

Embarrassed and looking slightly downward, he shook his head that it was indeed his soon to be ex-wife, Andrea who was out there. Patton took a deep breath and before opening the door, apologized. He said that he would be back if I wanted him to and as long as his daughter was okay.

As he opened the door, Andrea shouted piercingly as she pointed toward a double-parked car in front of my place. "Our daughter is sick with a fever and you are in there with some woman having sex?"

My mouth went agape and my eyebrows rose in astonishment at her audacity. I felt a bit like a guest from the Jerry Springer Show. It was almost comical if not disturbing.

"Where is she, where is Emilie?" Patton's voice was full of panic.

5

Andrea pointed to her car, a four-door Lexus sedan that I later learned Patton had purchased for her during their marriage. She was still ranting using some unrecognizable syllables and swearwords.

I shut the door and went upstairs to check on McKenna, but the unexpected disturbance had not awakened her.

Asleep, McKenna was as peaceful and beautiful as always. Filled with love, I petted her soft hair and smiled at her sleepy mouth.

I quickly had to get back to reality in case something else happened. What if that crazy woman came back with a gun? I went back downstairs, took a large gulp from my wine glass and just stood there in my dining room baffled. Into what was I potentially getting myself? I wondered what I would do if he did come back. I didn't have an answer.

Once again, I heard a knock at the door. I didn't know what to say to him. But when I opened the door, Andrea was standing there.

Far from coming to apologize, Andrea was in a rage! With threatening eyes, she waved her bony finger at my face. "You stay the hell away from my daughter you fucking bitch!" She walked toward her car and I quickly shut and locked my front door. I had never, ever, been talked like that; I was speechless!

Wait! Where was Patton? What if she did something horrific to him? I found the crumbly piece of paper with his number scribbled on it and dialed. No answer, just voicemail.

Just as I hung up, I heard another knock on the door. Scared, I went to the window upstairs, to peek out before I answered. It was Patton. When I opened the door, he was surprisingly cool but definitely remorseful about Andrea's visit.

"I am so sorry that happened. My daughter is not sick but I understand if you don't want me to come back in." Patton reasoned.

I couldn't understand how he could remain so calm and I went with my impulse and welcomed him back. I had been in possessive relationships before and I could truly empathize with him.

I guess Patton felt he either owed me an explanation or that I wanted one by the expression on my face.

"I told you how she came to my office and clocked me in the face when we were married for only a month. I really wanted to leave the marriage but I felt like I had to at least try to make it work. I attempted to make it work for a few more months but the games she played just got to me. The last time Andrea lured me back we had already separated a few times. She still had the lease on her apartment and would go there. Then she would apologize and I would forgive her. I felt sorry for her. She had a rotten life, or at least she professed to have. I guess I just wanted to fix her and make her happy"

Patton paused to look at my reaction I suppose to decide if he should expound further. I looked at him empathetically and told him to go on.

"Well, most of the times when she would try to make things up to me, she was a great wife. She didn't work so she would clean and cook and do the bills, you know household things. When I was happy with her, we would you know, sleep together. It was a Friday when we had our final argument and I was finally ready to give up on our marriage for good and go down to the courthouse to file. Nothing was going to stop me and I was going to do it first thing Monday morning when the courthouse opened. In fact, as a threat to me, she had done that herself once a couple of months before that fight, thinking she would rattle my cage and encourage me to work harder to make her happy. She even took all of my clothes and threw them in the front yard of our house! A week later she withdrew her (divorce) petition but this time, *I* was going to do it no matter what she said or did." He spoke with defeat and exhaustion, I could feel the tension with every word he shared.

He continued. "That Sunday morning Andrea called me pleading for me to come over because she was sick. I took some food over to her apartment and left. She called me again later that day and begged me to come back and take her to the hospital. It was there, in the emergency room, that the doctor informed us that Andrea was pregnant."

I felt like I had just lived through the whole exasperating saga with him. "Oh my gosh! What were you feeling, I mean were you happy or angry or what?"

Patton barely smiled as he told me, "Andrea looked at me and asked if I was happy. My parents raised me to do the right thing. I decided to try to make the marriage work for our unborn child. I believe children deserved to be raised with both a mother and a father. My own parents had been married for almost forty-five years! I thought that maybe Andrea's insecurities would be alleviated now that she was carrying our child. I bought a home on the water here in St. Petersburg and hoped to start over with her"

Sadly for Patton, Andrea never changed; he said that she was even worse when she was pregnant. And after Emilie was born, when she was still very young, Patton told me that Andrea "was out of her mind," the worst that he had ever experienced. He left and moved in with a friend, Jim, for almost half a year. When Patton moved back in with Andrea and his daughter for one final effort, for his daughter's sake, Andrea wouldn't let him sleep. She threw objects and her fists at Patton leaving holes in the walls. When Patton locked himself in various rooms in the house, she kicked and kicked until the door had holes in it. He hated that Emilie, at just a year old, was exposed to such an unhealthy relationship and environment so he moved out for good after officially filing for divorce in early 2002.

Getting back to the present, neither Patton nor I could figure out how Andrea knew that he had been at my house that night. Emilie was only two so she couldn't have remembered the address even if her mother did prod her. Andrea must have spied on him. I pitied Patton; he seemed like such a nice guy to have to deal with so much jealousy and instability.

A little more wine and deeper sharing, brought us closer, close enough to be passionately kissing.

That was our official first date. I prayed Andrea's visit wasn't indicative of what was to come. When Patton left that evening, I talked to God. I asked Him to guide me. Should I stop there and never see Patton again to avoid any future confrontations with his ex or should I wait and see? Maybe this was just a one-time deal? I had always heard that we meet people or God puts people in our lives for a reason. His divorce would be final shortly so all that drama seemed likely to pass.

I went upstairs again to look at my beauty, sleeping like an angel without a care in the world. How blessed I was that she was mine. I loved her more than I had ever loved anyone or ever would. Motherhood is the greatest possible gift from God, I thought. I smiled and lifted her sleeping body from her bed and held her against me while she slept. Her head was over my shoulder, her slightly sweaty hair smelled so sweet, her skin so delicate and soft, I began to meld into her breathing and my worries about Patton dissipated, for a while anyway.

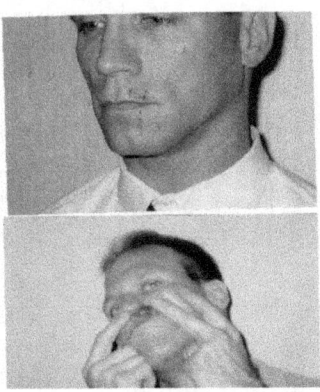 

Patton, after one month of marriage to Andrea.   Patton and Emilie in 2003.

9

Love is patient, love is kind.
  1 Corinthians 13:4

II: Moving Forward?

My house was on the market for less than four months, and I sold it exactly for what I was asking. The profit allowed me to purchase a larger house with a yard and an oversized garage. I had enough left over to do some interior construction and refurbishing.

Patton took time out of his weekend to help me move, informing me that his now ex-wife just bought a house about four blocks away from my new place just a couple of months before then. What? I wished I would have known sooner.

It was still too early in our relationship to assess the potential. But we were starting to create memories, and I was falling harder for him.

Patton's positive demeanor, witty comebacks, and kind heart won me over. He was, and still remains, every bit the person I thought he was from day one. He had everything and more than I was looking for. Patton was a mature, morally sound, honest, Christian, athletic, loving, and intelligent man. He was an adoring father who would do anything for his daughter.

During our two-year courtship, we had only sporadic gatherings that would include both of our daughters, like McKenna's fourth birthday party. That was where Emilie first sported an unexplained black eye that Patton said Emilie told him came from "playing" at her mother's house.

Andrea had been keeping her distance the first few months following their divorce but then just as we were comfortably enjoying peace, she kicked it into overdrive.

One evening Patton and I were driving to go out for a romantic dinner when Andrea's voice called out to him. His phone doubled as a two-way radio. Andrea was just out of a relationship with a doctor she had dated and had started to call to Patton regularly. She sounded needy. Fact or fiction, she would come up with some reason to call or attempt to see him. I had no doubt that he wasn't romantically interested in her anymore since my first brief impression of her had been a lasting one.

Patton answered her call, turned off the speaker and switched it to regular phone mode. He answered a few questions with brief yes or no answers. He ended the call, saying he was busy and would contact her the following day.

When Patton and I arrived at the trendy, yet sparsely populated restaurant, he put his cell phone on the table. With apprehension, I asked if he wouldn't mind turning it off. He said he would prefer to keep it on just in case any emergency happened with Emilie. I admired his love for his daughter but felt just a little resentful that I couldn't have one straight hour of peace at the dinner table.

He left it on.

The second phone call from Andrea came with our appetizers. He took the call. Although I couldn't hear her, it was clear from his responses that she was inquiring what he was doing. He said he was having dinner and would call her back tomorrow.

But her inquisition didn't end there. She was clearly asking for details as he fired off answers, "It's not important," "--It doesn't matter," before finally closing out the call.

Andrea called five more times during our dinner date although Patton did not take those calls. By the time he took me home, I was feeling annoyed. I didn't want to sound as crazy as Andrea, but I didn't want to enable or encourage this as acceptable behavior. My mom was keeping McKenna at her place for the night and although I was looking forward to Patton staying over, I was not in a positive mood. I told him that I had to get up early and it wasn't a good night to stay. I thanked him for dinner and kissed him good night before he drove away.

11

A couple of days later, Patton called and told me he was sorry about the calls. He said he would tell Andrea that unless it was about Emilie, and important, to refrain from calling him on his cell phone in the evening or to just leave a message. I was happy to hear of his proposed solution.

During our two years of dating, Patton and I had celebrated many memorable occasions. We had gone to New York on a trip I earned through my work. I arranged and planned his surprise fortieth birthday. We often visited his parents who lived four hours away and we started sharing some holidays together. It was close to McKenna's fifth birthday when Patton proposed. Six months later we married.

Do nothing from rivalry or conceit, but in humility count others more significant than yourselves. Let each of you look not only to his own interests, but also to the interests of others.

Philippians 2:3-4

III: Garage Garbage

Patton told me I didn't have to work after we got married, so I didn't! I looked forward to the break and really wanted to focus on mothering and being a good wife to my new husband. I would be updating the house he purchased on the water three years prior (back when he was trying to make his marriage work with Andrea since she was pregnant with his child).

The house was unintentionally retro, and needed a very deep cleaning which surprised me since Andrea had been living in the home alone with their baby for several months while they were separated. She didn't work yet the floors and counters were filthy. Emilie's dried baby vomit was encrusted in more than a dozen places and the dust was so thick it created a new finish to the top surfaces of the few remaining pieces of unloved furniture Andrea didn't take. The entire interior needed painting, and the house itself smelled musty. I certainly had my work cut out for me but fortunately, I loved to decorate, paint and get things in order so I had no complaints.

Although the home needed TLC, it was in a prestigious neighborhood and on the open water facing east with a true million-dollar view. Patton got an amazing deal on it but in Florida, regardless of how long you are married, if the home was acquired during the marriage, the equity had to be split 50/50. Andrea received a check for $178,000 even though she spent less than a year under the same roof with Patton.

With the profit of close to $60,000 from the sale of my home I was able to comfortably decorate and help furnish our home over the next few months.

After getting on a pretty regular housewife schedule, I was found additional time for volunteering. Prior to our marriage, I had assisted once or twice a week in McKenna's first grade classroom but now that I wasn't working anymore, I could give more. I asked Patton if it would be okay to also help out in Emilie's kindergarten classroom (at another school) since he wasn't able to often, due to his less flexible attorney hours. Additionally, I wanted to take the opportunity to check into the school Emilie attended as a possibility for McKenna's enrollment the following school year. Although both of our girls were enrolled in private Christian schools, it would be ideal for them to attend the same one since the holiday break times at each respective school were not completely in sync. Patton agreed it was fine. I signed up to volunteer at Emilie's Christian school. The teacher asked me if I'd like to help on a regular basis so I committed to do so, but just once a month because I didn't want to overstep my role as Emilie's stepmother.

A few weeks later, when I arrived in Emilie's classroom for the first time, she looked surprised and happy to see me. I only stayed about an hour that day but was glad to have some time with her, watching her learn and interact outside of the home with her peers. She seemed to fit in well and the school had all the children reading at an impressive level. In fact the curriculum there appeared to be what McKenna had used the year before when she as in kindergarten. Although, McKenna was almost eleven months older than Emilie, she was technically supposed to be in the same grade as her stepsister, but McKenna was tested and advanced to the next grade level the year before.

Three weeks after I volunteered for Emilie's class, McKenna and I went to a Target store after school to pick up some decorations and needs for McKenna's birthday sleepover party at our house the following night. After I put the bags in the rear hatch of my new Nissan Pathfinder, I got McKenna secured into her car seat and looked down at my phone; I had six missed calls from Andrea.

Arriving home and pulling into my garage, I noticed a pair of headlights right behind me. Startled, I looked in my rear view mirror to see Emilie, and a very angry looking Andrea, getting out of her car. I was speaking on my cell phone to Cathy, the mother of one of McKenna's friends, so before I opened the car door to get out, I quickly asked her to stay on the phone, whispering, "My husband's ex-wife has been stalking me by phone and just pulled up to my house. I am scared of this woman, she is crazy!"

I could almost hear Cathy's confused gasp. Who could blame her? After she cleared her throat not knowing what to say, she offered instead for her daughter, Caitlyn, to get on the phone with McKenna and talk about the upcoming party. I gave the phone to McKenna who I ushered into the house quickly as I followed her in to turn off the alarm. I stalled as long as I could before going back into the garage. When I opened the door, Emilie was walking toward me to go inside with McKenna.

"Stop, Emilie, do not go in there!" Andrea yelled. "What I have to say I want you to hear. Your stepmother is a liar, and I want you to see what a liar she is!" Was she kidding me? What was happening?

I was terribly frightened! Patton wasn't home yet and I had no idea of what Andrea was capable.

She squinted her green eyes into a pair of maniacal looking black marbles. "I need to talk to you right now!"

"Andrea, please let Emilie go inside so she doesn't have to see you yell like this." I suggested calmly. I had no idea what had gotten her so fired up but my heart was racing and I could feel the color draining from my face.

As Andrea insisted that Emilie stay out there with us,

McKenna opened the door to ask if she could come in to the garage with me. She seemed to want to protect me. But I insisted she go back in right away. I couldn't expose my child to such a verbally heated brawl.

The palms of my hands were perspiring profusely and I was visibly trembling but I needed to show strength and confidence. I felt myself inconspicuously trying to take a few deep breaths to calm my nerves.

I looked directly at Andrea and saw nothing but evil. She ranted on. "You said when you and Patton got married you would NOT overstep your boundaries! You LIED!" She yelled at me, standing next to her wide-eyed, petrified-looking daughter.

I attempted to reply calmly. "Andrea, please, I am begging you to let Emilie go inside with McKenna and not listen to this."

"No! I want her to hear this!" She raged.

"I didn't overstep my boundaries, Andrea. What are you talking about?" I was losing my patience.

"You told me that you weren't going to volunteer at Emilie's school and the principal called me today and told me that you volunteered there!" She furrowed her brow, crinkled her upper and lower eyelids together and moved a step closer to intimidate me. She succeeded but I tried not to show her how nervous and frightened I was.

She stammered and spit her way into her next sentence. "Emilie doesn't want you to volunteer; she wants me, her mother to, not you! Emilie, who do you want to volunteer at school, Mommy or Lisa?" She barely took a breath as she delivered the leading question to her terrified five-year old. Emilie just looked at her mom's face while she lifted up her arm slowly to point to Andrea.

"See!" Andrea was sounding like a child now.

I couldn't help myself; I had to teach her Parenting 101. "First of all, you do not need to let your five-year-old daughter see all of this. Please let her go inside. Or you go cool down and call me later so we can talk privately."

16

While she stumbled for a way to respond to my calm directive, I added, "If you don't calm down now, I want you to at least leave my property."

"No! I will leave when I am good and ready! I want my daughter to hear what a liar you are!"

After thinking quickly about what she had said, I barreled back to her. "Oh okay, so the school called you today to tell you, 'Hey Andrea, you know, Lisa volunteered three weeks ago for an hour and we just wanted to call you three weeks later to let you know.' Are you kidding me? They didn't do that! And you are calling me a liar? Do you even know how to tell the truth, Andrea?" As I was asking the question, I wondered how confrontational she would become calling her out in a lie.

She didn't deny it, she just went on as if I had said nothing at all! "You lied because you said you wouldn't overstep the boundaries and volunteer at her school and you did! How would you like it if I volunteered at McKenna's school?" she shouted.

Shaking my head, I chuckled condescendingly. "If you want to go and volunteer at *my* daughter's school, help yourself! She's not your stepdaughter so I am sure they would love an outsider to come and help them for free." I didn't like confrontation but was pleased I was able to quickly respond with a rational answer.

Again, I must have stumped her since she changed subjects instantly, it was as if she didn't hear me at all. "You think you are so hot driving in your new car with your fake boobs and poufy lips! You aren't hot, you are so ugly!" Aha! This was the real story. To reinforce it, she moved closer and pointed that long boney finger in my face that I remembered from my notorious first date with Patton. "You hear me, you are UGLY! Look at all those acne scars on your face! You are trying to over compensate with those fake boobs."

I could no longer contain myself. Andrea's decibel and nasty tone, plus the fact that she had physically pushed herself into me and my personal space in the garage made me both in fear for my life and enraged. I put on my best poker face as I once again tried to end her outburst. "Andrea, I have asked you to leave and asked that Emilie not hear this, but you don't care what you are doing to your own daughter. You want to talk about my fake boobs? Mine are B's and your fake boobs are D's – and thanks for the compliments on my lips! As far as being ugly, I guess Patton doesn't think so, he married me and loves me; he thinks I am beautiful!" I could feel my hands trembling and a hot red color returning to my cheeks. I was infuriated.

"He doesn't love you! He's cheating on you! He and all his friends hate you! I talk to his friends every day and they all hate you!" She was not backing down.

I noticed Emilie's face. She was standing there blank-faced with her mouth agape, looking completely lost. "Andrea, please let Emilie go inside so she doesn't have to hear and see all this!"

"No!" she stomped like a toddler.

Just as she did, McKenna came into the garage and threw her hands over each of Emilie's ears, as she said sadly, "Emilie, come inside, don't listen to this! Your mom is lying!"

While I appreciated McKenna looking out for Emilie, I didn't want her to be exposed to this crazy nonsense, either. "McKenna, thank you and that is sweet, but please go back inside." McKenna obediently reentered the house.

"Andrea, please get off my property and don't say another word. You need to get help and talk to someone." I said half threatening and half concerned.

"No, I will leave when I am good and ready!" She vented.

I was at a loss of options but to resort to what I believed to be the crux of her animosity. "Okay. I just don't know what else it could be, Andrea, but jealousy. So, please just go get some counseling." I finally spewed out.

"Jealous, of you? I am not jealous of you! I don't need counseling! You do! And this isn't your property, it is Patton's!"

I was calmer now and although my hands were still perspiring, they were less shaky. I gave her my final admonition. "No, this is my property too; my name is now on the mortgage so get off of *our* property before I call the police." I was confident I was sending a message that I refused to back down and that I wouldn't allow someone like her to get the best of me. Patton and I had just finished refinancing our house and my name really was on the deed.

The threat of police must have worked because she finally left the garage and started walking toward her car. But she had to get the last words in. "I'll leave but I will see you proven unfit!" she threatened while she sidestepped away. Grabbing Emilie's hand, she screamed, "And Emilie doesn't love you, she loves me and hates you!"

After they left and I closed the garage door. Inside the house, I turned the home alarm on and called my husband at work. Shaken and almost unable to speak, my teeth chattered and my body quivered as I told him every detail of the previous ten minutes. I wanted him to get a restraining order against her, but he said he needed to think what would be best to do for Emilie's sake.

Still shaken after we hung up the phone, I remembered that I had the party things in the car and needed to get my mind back on track. I had been pretty excited about the party for McKenna. I went back into the garage and when I reached to open the hatch of my car I noticed about a twenty-inch long key mark in the paint of the back door of my SUV. I was shocked as I noticed the little clump of freshly piled scraped paint at the end of the scratch.

(Ch.3 Fig.1)

It was clearly noticeable now when I opened the door. I had opened it at Target to put in bags and get out tissue two hours or so prior so I would have noticed it then, too. But it hadn't been there. Andrea must have done it when I went inside with McKenna to turn off the alarm. What else was this woman capable of?

By the next morning, I had cooled off. This was going to be my life for at least the next thirteen years until Emilie went off to college and her child support stopped.

I had to attempt to make it right. For all of our sakes, I had no choice but to extend an olive branch and make peace with Andrea.

I called Andrea that morning and told her how I never wanted to relive the prior night with her again. I told her how I noticed the key-mark on my car and was still willing to make a fresh start with her and not volunteer in Emilie's class anymore knowing how upset it made her.

Her response to my gesture and forgiveness?

"You are a liar and I have nothing to say to you." Click, she hung up.

What was wrong with this woman? She was clearly deficient, mentally. Who behaved like this? This wasn't just jealousy; this was something far more insidious.

To my chagrin, after giving it much thought, Patton decided that a restraining order would not be a good idea as it would complicate things and embarrass his daughter if ever Andrea's and my paths were to cross, such as at the grocery store. I did not agree. It was not okay for her to treat me like this and get away with it! His decision enabled her to repeat her monstrous acts because there were no consequences to Andrea.

I contemplated ending our marriage. I was in fear of my life and I longed to go back to the more simple days of just me and McKenna.

I decided to give it another chance since we had only been married for six months and I felt that God would be disappointed in me for not trying hard enough. After all, our vows included, "for better and for worse."

Still, I prayed that things would improve.

As for a person who stirs up division, after warning him once and then twice, have nothing more to do with him.
  Titus 3-10

IV: The Road to Change

Emilie's visitation with Patton was every other weekend (Friday through Sunday) plus Mondays and Wednesdays after school until 8 p.m. The weekend of the garage incident was a weekend with her mother. So, we did not see her until that Monday.

Even though I was happy to see Emilie sitting gleefully at the kitchen counter after Patton brought her home from school, her blunt and matter-of-fact announcement, "I don't love you, Lisa," certainly caught me off guard.

Instead of admonishing her, I challenged her to think about what she had just said by asking her a simple question. "Really? Why don't you love me anymore, Emilie?" I used a slightly sad tone and frowned lips to make her realize that it hurt my feelings. I wasn't sure if this was a good thing to do or not. Had Emilie retained this information after she heard her mother say it in the garage or had Andrea drilled it in to her head all weekend? What exactly prompted this?

She answered, "Because my mom told me that I don't love you anymore." There it was, blatant alienation.

Patton quickly jumped in, as did McKenna. They told Emilie to choose from her heart not from words of another person. McKenna, more defensively, asked her how she could listen to her mother tell her such things after all that I had done for her.

Emilie looked a little mischievous, "I know, I still love you, Lisa." She then apologized after her father asked her to and we went on with our evening.

Patton contacted Andrea by phone when his visitation was over. He told her that Emilie had said some "mean things" when she came over and asked her to stop trying to influence their daughter's feelings about who she loved.

Andrea vehemently denied ever saying such a thing and added, "Lisa was the confrontational one who was yelling and screaming at me in the garage!"

Patton pointed out to Andrea that she was in *our* garage and called her out by telling her that she often reversed the story putting herself as the victim and the person whom she victimized as the perpetrator.

I was happy to hear my husband take my side even as she continued to attempt an emotional pity plea from him. Thankfully, this time he didn't succumb.

About a month following that phone call, Andrea lost her job at a mortgage company with whom she was employed for a couple of months. This wasn't surprising; she seemed unable to hold any position for very long. The longest period I recall her holding a job since I met my husband was at Lifestyles' Gym where she sold memberships. That was a good outlet for her. She had plenty of new victims from which to choose and share her twisted lies about Patton and how "he abused her and didn't pay child support." She also seemed obsessed with working out. In fact, she would work out at Gold's Gym, then an hour later, go a mile away to Lifestyles to work out again.

I learned this after my own workout at Gold's. Around eight o'clock in the evening, I went into the child care center to pick McKenna up and saw Emilie. "Why are you still wearing your school uniform; haven't you been home yet?" I asked her.

"No, my mom picked me up from school and we went to Lifestyles and then came here." She innocently answered.

If her mom had picked her up at closing of school's aftercare program at six o'clock, Emilie had not had any time with her mother or at home since that morning.

My husband had begged, literally begged Andrea, for precious time like this with Emilie. Any time Andrea wasn't available, he had asked her to please just call him and he would drop everything especially since our house was just five minutes from the gym and about eight from her house.

Andrea refused to let Patton see his own child outside of his designated minimum visitation hours. More importantly, she deprived her own daughter of time and love from her father.

Patton and I added the gym conversation with Emilie to the computer journal we had begun keeping since the garage incident. Documenting almost became a job in and of itself as the frequency of alienation and questionable events began to increase exponentially.

For example, there were two student performance events scheduled at Emilie's school that year. The Christmas Program and the Spring Program were to showcase the hard work and creativity by the students musically, artistically, and biblically. They were super adorable and very entertaining. The performances generally lasted for only an hour. The children were even graded: attend and get 100% or be absent (sans illness) and get a zero. That first Christmas program, when Emilie was just in kindergarten, she received a zero because she never showed.

The functions always took place on Tuesdays because that was when the school's cathedral was available to hold a large audience. Tuesday was Andrea's time with Emilie. She only had one kindergarten Christmas performance in her lifetime and her absence really seemed to break Patton's spirit. He called Andrea several times from outside of the cathedral, but she wouldn't answer.

Andrea had put her destructive alienation tactics toward my husband ahead of Emilie's best interests. (We later found out she had taken Emilie to a domestic violence counselor that very afternoon. Andrea was starting to build a story, a web of lies about Patton, suggesting he was abusing Emilie.)

The Spring Program was better since Emilie was actually present! However, the tension at this and all future performances became our new "normal". Emilie showed up for the bi-annual performances but was typically not correctly attired or perhaps a bit sloppy. She looked uncomfortable, too, not her usual happy self.

She also began to develop mannerisms, looking away when Patton or I made eye contact (sometimes even frowning in a nasty way) and fidgeting with her hands while she was not performing. When Patton and I approached to take a picture of/with her after the finale, Andrea would get to her first and scoop her up like the church was aflame. It was pitiful. As we left the building, Emilie's artwork that had been on display earlier in the vestibule was missing. Andrea took and kept any piece of joy from Patton that she could.

As a pleasant surprise, however, a few days after the Christmas Program (the year that Emilie, missed it) Andrea relinquished her time with Emilie for the entire Christmas break through January fourth. Andrea said she was going to Las Vegas with her on-and-off-again boyfriend, Dr. Hank.

Andrea knew how to find nice men, especially if they had a well-paying career. To her credit, she always seemed to find the compassionate, naïve, men who would easily fall for her victimization stories; just the way Patton had. I secretly hoped that Dr. Hank would sweep her off her feet and marry her in a Vegas chapel. Maybe then the saga of her revenge against Patton (and me) would finally end.

Unfortunately, Dr. Hank's plan wasn't to sweep Andrea off her feet. We never learned the reason but Andrea was actually back in town a couple of days early. We were at a Chili's restaurant when we received Andrea's call. Patton handed the phone to Emilie and her mother said she was home early and asked who she wanted to stay with that night. We had had her for almost two weeks so I wouldn't have been surprised if she wanted to go to her mom's, but she didn't.

"I want to stay with Daddy for one more night and then tomorrow I will see you," Emilie told her mother before they hung up.

Not two minutes later, Andrea called back and demanded Patton to bring Emilie her home right away. "We have just gotten our food," Patton responded. "I'll bring Emilie to your house as soon as we finish." Patton didn't often argue with Andrea, especially in front of his daughter. He wanted to eliminate stress in her life and anticipated that Andrea's voice on the phone indicated that Emilie was in for something when she got back to her mom's. He frequently reminded me, "I have lived with the woman, and I know how she takes her stress out on whomever she is around!"

Emilie was very upset. "She told me I could stay another night! She is MEAN!" She sniffled and teared between stuttered speech.

Poor thing, I thought to myself as I nodded in my disbelief. It was nearly eight at night, why would Andrea care if she had Emilie home that night or the following morning? She hadn't cared about giving this year's Christmas vacation to us. Could it be that she actually missed her daughter?

Andrea offered no explanation. She told Patton it was a Monday and Emilie was due home at eight before she hung up on him.

My mind was racing with questions. Did Dr. Hank break up with her? Would the next day, week, month or year be horrendous for us because she and Dr. Hank weren't together anymore? Would she continue to use Emilie as a pawn or was this a stress related decision? When you hear your little girl crying about going home after she tells you she is having fun and wants one more night with her daddy, how can you deny them? Something was up.

With almost none of Andrea's antics to document since the Christmas program we enjoyed record peace time (about three-and-a-half weeks). We feared the end of that special time had come. Sadly, we were right!

Patton dropped Emilie off at her mother's house one night soon after the Chili's evening and Andrea told Patton there would no longer be any more overnights on Mondays and Wednesdays and for him not to bathe Emilie any more before slamming the door in his face.

After she did, Patton used his cell phone to call Andrea once he entered his car. "That is the kind of behavior our daughter sees and learns..." Andrea hung up on him mid-sentence. A few minutes passed and as she often did, especially when her child support payment was due, she called back.

Patton refused to take her calls on his cell phone or at our house later since she slammed the door and refused to speak to him by phone about it. But Andrea's persistence finally got the best of me so I answered only to tell her that Patton had nothing to say to her at the moment.

Andrea spoke in her cunning, soft manipulative, voice. "I need to speak with him." Pause. "It's nothing bad, it's positive. It's about Emilie."

Patton said no; he would call her back tomorrow.

She did not like that and began to get out of control on the phone, so I hung up on her. In the next two hours, we counted twenty-three calls before we finally turned off the ringers and took a photo of the Caller-ID verifying her harassment.

To my dismay, the next day, Andrea contacted Patton on his cell phone mid-day when I wasn't with him. This time he apparently did more than just accept her call; he spoke with her extensively! I couldn't understand why given all that had happened the night before. I was upset about him yet again enabling her. I saw that vicious cycle to which he often fell prey.

Patton told me about the conversation and her slippery charm which was always absent of an apology. He reminded me again that he didn't care why Andrea acted the way she did; he just wanted her to be happy so that she would give him more time with his daughter and also so that she wouldn't take her rage out on Emilie. As much as I admired that, I couldn't help loathe the broken records of justification. It pushed me away, and I felt disrespected.

I tried to accept that Emilie was and always would be his priority. I encouraged him to think that easily forgiving Andrea every time she behaved improperly or said something inappropriate, she would be teaching Emilie that she could do the same.

Patton was usually very forthcoming to me about his conversations with her so he did share the details. The long and short of it was that Andrea had opened up and confided in Patton that she still had some "unresolved feelings" for him and wanted to know if he truly had moved on.

She was just in Las Vegas with Dr. Hank and Patton and I were married, not dating. I was angry and confused. I knew she didn't have feelings for my husband because in my mind she was a sociopath, someone who was incapable of true "feelings," especially love; they merely fake their emotions to gain something.

Patton said he actually felt badly for her. He thought she was hurt. She was upset when he told her that he had truly moved on. He pointed out that he had been married to me for almost a year and that they would never get back together again. He said he had to tell her flatly because she didn't seem to accept his testimony to our marriage. She then resumed her angry tone and talked over him before hanging up on him.

It wasn't long before Patton picked Emilie up for his next visitation. He was planning to take her to her t-ball practice. Andrea refused to give Patton the hat and team shirt that was part of Emilie's uniform. She used it as leverage as she held Emilie back at the door saying that Emilie didn't want to go with him and hated him. She spoke violently. "She hates the way you treat me, Patton.

She said she is tired of seeing you trying to hurt me and scream at me!" Andrea continuously accused others of things she did; a common alienation strategy. We were uncertain if she believed her own lies or if she was simply trying to make herself look like the victim while getting pity.

Running late for practice, Patton reached in and took Emilie's hand and drove off to the field. Andrea followed them in her car to the parking lot at the playing field where she screamed and made a scene in front of the other parents and children. It had to be humiliating to Emilie and was certainly embarrassing for Patton. A coach later said to him that he had seen that kind of thing before but not to worry; they were not judging Emilie and she was always welcome there.

Days later, Patton, McKenna and I picked Emilie up from her mother's house in the morning to take her to soccer practice and a game for a neighborhood recreational team. Patton had signed her up after Emilie expressed an interest. She seemed to like soccer as much as the t-ball and was an amazingly strong and natural athlete. She was dedicated and motivated like a champion player would be. Thankfully, her muscles and agility helped her to do incredibly well considering her mother rarely took her to practice or games that fell on her days or weekends. Patton would tell the coach, he was sorry she wasn't there during her mother's weekends but promised that he would continue to try to get her mother to take her. Per usual, the coaches were great with children that age. They understood that sometimes families had conflicts that could prohibit them from attending practices or games.

We asked Emilie if her mom would be coming to the soccer game. "No," she said, adding that she had asked her mother, "if it was because Lisa was going?"

Andrea answered, "It is too awkward. You and I will do something special later when you get back." But, there was no "later". Andrea called Patton shortly after the game to tell us we could keep her that night. I somehow

29

felt that was easier for her than keeping her promise of doing something special with Emilie. Emilie often said she never did anything at her mom's except watch TV or go to the child care center at the gym.

Because I felt badly for her, I would occasionally try to point out something optimistic. "Your mommy takes you to a nail salon to get your nails polished, that must be fun, right?"

Emilie was both sad and frustrated when she replied. "She only takes me because she has to go all the time to get filled."

Emilie's words and her expressions begged for her mother's attention and love. It was so sad to see this child, who I grew to love more each day, with a broken heart at such a young age.

Each drop off was an instant replay of the last. Andrea would never really acknowledge Emilie coming home. She just let her in while hiding behind her front door as if it was some kind of privilege to see her. Then she'd stick her drawn, sallow face through the small opening while yelling about something, anything, to try to argue with Patton as if to make him look combative. She slammed the door as a final touch.

Emilie saw, learned, and later, mimicked those types of behaviors and mannerisms. Andrea initially welcomed it when Patton called to speak with his daughter because the few self-serving calls she took, gave her the opportunity to have a one-sided phone conversation in which Emilie could only hear her mom acting like a victim. "Stop talking to me like that in front of our daughter..." He finally reduced the amount of times he would try to speak to his daughter by phone.

Although I was feeling as agitated as he was, I felt more removed and uninvolved, like I wasn't a part of this strange dysfunctional life we were living. I felt like an outsider looking in.

Patton was getting closer to taking legal action against Andrea in the best interests of Emilie but Florida's custody modification statute was stringent and incredibly subjective. He wanted to be certain he could win his case before he invested his time and money, and worried about Andrea's instability upon being served. The lies and manipulations continued as did our mounting documentation including video and audio recordings of her outbursts.

For I know the plans I have for you, declares the Lord, plans for welfare and not for evil, to give you a future and a hope.
Jeremiah 29:11

V: What's Wrong with Andrea?

Emilie, at six years old, was now at an age where she began to emulate Andrea, perhaps subconsciously.

We saw in Emilie's behavior, for example, more euphoria at the end and beginning of each month. There was an undeniable pattern. It didn't take long for us to draw the correlation since it coincided with her mother receiving her child support money from Patton which was due the first day of each month yet Patton often paid a few days early.

As I mentioned, Andrea didn't work often if she chose to work at all. She was living off of her child support, which of course is non-taxable income. She even used the education tax credit on her taxes although Patton was the one who paid 100% of Emilie's private school. When we married I found that he had initially sent the school tuition in the form a check made out to Andrea and she would cut the check to the school. I asked him to instead pay the school directly so he would be able to receive the credit and he took my advice, yet Andrea continued to take the write-off. She had no expenses for Emilie. All of her debts were standard living expenses whether she had a child or not such as her mortgage, car, cell phone or electric, for example.

Anything that related directly to Emilie was paid for willingly by Patton. Emilie's school lunches, summer camps, health insurance, doctor office co-pays, pre-paid college tuition plan, all school fees and tuitions, uniforms, supplies, instrument rental and lessons, reading books, sports lessons and uniforms, golf clubs, running shoes, field trips, were just a few of his extra expenses on top of Andrea's support. I couldn't help but resent Andrea for refusing to assist in these costs. In fact, I resented my husband for enabling her. I reminded repeatedly him the first few years of our marriage that the more he gave in, the more Andrea, would expect and demand it.

But I too, wanted Emilie to have all the niceties that she would have had if she was living with us full-time and grew to accept Andrea would never chip in.

One month when Andrea received her support early from Patton, she was almost blissful based on the tone of her voice and the very rare occasion when she offered a few extra hours for Patton to spend time with Emilie. But, her happiness dulled the moment she learned we were going to enroll McKenna in the same school that Emilie attended. She went ballistic!

Andrea called Patton and announced that she, "couldn't take being that close geographically." She told him that she was going to sell her house and move away. To deter her and set her straight, Patton reminded Andrea that their Marital Settlement Agreement (MSA) precluded her from moving with Emilie except to one of the two adjacent counties.

Patton attempted to calmly reason with Andrea, pointing out that Emilie was happy and successful at her school and that she loved the local t-ball and soccer teams on which she played, so Andrea's idea of moving out of the county was clearly for spite.

Andrea reiterated that she didn't care and was going to move. Later on one of the many voice mails we saved to use against her in court, she demanded it be "put in writing that McKenna wasn't going to Emilie's school."

"You do what you have to do and I'll do what I have to do!" Patton warned her.

The War of the Youngs had now begun!

After a year of marriage, I thanked God that Patton finally stood up to Andrea! Maybe there was hope that we could focus on being a happy family without so much tension in our lives.

I believed that putting his foot down might truly effect a change one way or the other. Andrea would either reveal her evil puppetry and get herself arrested or she would have to play nice now that Patton indicated he would be doing "whatever he had to do," for Emilie. Either way, things would surely be less contentious? Considering that Andrea refused to pay for even a three dollar school field trip or two dollar spiral notebook, she wouldn't dare jeopardize her hefty child support by risking a custody dispute.

A few days later, at the next soccer practice to which we took Emilie, we saw Andrea on the sideline. We had never seen Andrea at any of the practices or games. Andrea wasn't alone, she was with a friend. I had also never seen her with a friend, ever! I felt strangely encouraged as the fresh air seemed to cultivate my hope and faith in her.

I decided to go and say hello to Andrea to see how she'd respond, praying it would be favorably. I supposed it was the right thing to do, we were in public and I felt safe from her forked tongue knowing her friend might also serve as a sort of buffer. Andrea shocked me when she reciprocated my greeting in kind! I then introduced myself to her friend who jovially told me her name was "Romaine, like the lettuce."

Boasting a genuinely contagious smile, I felt instantly comfortable with Romaine. She looked to come from a multi-cultural background as her skin was a warm cinnamon brown and her eyes big and bright. Her face illuminated when I noticed her pretty jewelry and complimented it. She told me she made it all herself. I was impressed and asked her if she might make a certain piece for me as a gift to one of my friends. We exchanged phone numbers with a promise to contact each other.

The temperatures were dropping and Andrea mentioned how cold she was. As a strange sort of olive branch, I offered her an extra fleece jacket that I brought. It was surreal, us being kind to one another! Andrea wearing my jacket? Who would have ever expected that? Even McKenna, who had not been in Andrea's presence since the garage incident, seemed comfortable.

After Emilie's practice, as the sun was going down, we departed in separate directions. Andrea left with no goodbye, and Patton led me, with McKenna and Emilie holding each of my hands, while we walked toward our car.

"That was nice of my mom to come to my game," Emilie said when we were all in the car and heading home.

I agreed and said it was fun sitting with her mom and Romaine.

"But why didn't she say good bye to me?" Emilie asked enigmatically cocking her head slightly on an angle.

Per usual, Patton jumped in quickly. "I think she did on the field, honey, but she was with a friend and she was probably trying to let me have my weekend with you uninterrupted."

I know that in the decade I have known Emilie, I have seen only maybe a hug or two but not one kiss from her mother; it was so peculiar and sad. She wouldn't always voice it but you could frequently read my stepdaughter's eyes as her brows peaked at the center of her forehead; she was often melancholy when she spoke of her mother.

Within days, Andrea's alienating spirit returned. She resumed talking to Emilie about Patton and how it was his fault for the divorce. According to my stepdaughter, Andrea told her, "Daddy doesn't love you anymore…you aren't a part of his family" and "he has Lisa and McKenna now." It was so cruel. Where did that nice Andrea from the soccer field go?

I pondered and documented these comments, behaviors, events, and disturbing conversations. I was so baffled trying to understand the mechanics of why? Why would anyone do this? Why would a mother do this to her own child?

Although my own daughter had never met her biological father, I would absolutely have loved her to! I would have facilitated every possible meeting if he was interested. I cried for months after McKenna was born knowing that my daughter had a father who simply didn't want to be a part of her life.

John was punishing my daughter for something he blamed me for, ending our relationship. I drew the parallel with what Andrea was doing to Emilie. She was punishing Emilie for what she perceived as Patton's fault, their divorce.

Although I wouldn't go to any extreme of empowering Andrea, I deeply wanted this innocent little child to cease being Andrea's pawn. I might not have been able to help my own daughter with an abandoned father issue but I was going to try to help my stepdaughter and any others who I could if I exposed the reality of parental alienation by writing this book. When I started writing my story, I had no idea that these early years would pale in comparison to the horror to come.

Emilie avoiding eye contact with us as she gets ushered away by her mother at a school performance.

I tell you, on the Day of Judgment people will give account for every careless word they speak.
    Matthew 12:36

VI: Aspen, Baby!

Numerous calls in short spurts of time from Andrea had become the norm. Averaging twenty a day was no exaggeration. When her name appeared on the Caller ID more than two or three times, Patton and I would sometimes chuckle or more often, just shake our heads in disbelief of her audacity. To say she was persistent was an understatement. Andrea knew if she called frequently enough within a short period of time, Patton would eventually answer.

One day in January, she called about eight times in less than a half-hour. Patton wasn't home. What would this problem be? I tired of hearing the phone ring so I finally gave in and answered her ninth or tenth call.

Per usual, Andrea began in an urgent tone. "I need to speak to Patton!" She'd demand.

"Andrea, he is in trial today and when he gets out, I will have him call you." I was pacifying her just to keep the phone calls to a minimum for a while.

"I am completely against this honeymoon ski trip you have planned for spring break! Who goes on a honeymoon a year after they are married anyway, that is the stupidest thing I ever heard of!" She blew off steam, anyway.

I did not owe her an explanation but I did need peace. Maybe reducing some of her anxiety was the way to go, I thought.

I explained that the Aspen, Colorado trip was a wedding present from my father. I also tried to abate what I thought might be jealousy and reassured her that it doubled as family vacation and was not specifically a honeymoon. I told her how exciting it would be for Emilie to see snow and ski for the first time. (McKenna had gone with me to visit my father in Aspen before.) I tried to sound bubbly and excited to photograph and make video recordings of Emilie so I could share the clips with her.

Andrea's frustration did not wane. She wasn't getting off the phone quietly either. She decided swearing and volume would better suit her attempt to halt our plans.

"Goodbye Andrea, Patton will call you later." I hung up on her.

I thought about my stepdaughter and couldn't fathom being Emilie and having to live with a mother like that. I wondered if Emilie ever saw through her mother's manipulations or if she overheard her making that call, her obnoxious swearing and malicious tone as she had on so many phone calls. I wondered why Andrea cared where Emilie was going; this was her spring break, not Andrea's!

Since Emilie had begun to show signs of replicating her mother's opinions, I worried that she might suddenly say that she didn't want to go skiing. Coaching is a word frequently used when talking about parental alienation such as this; brainwashing is another.

Patton later returned Andrea's call and managed to calm her down and get her onboard with allowing Emilie to go on the ski trip. The crafty way of doing this was almost always money. Patton mentioned he was mailing in his child support the next morning so she would have it a week early.

But for the next few weeks, Andrea continued to vacillate back and forth about the Aspen trip up until the very day before we were to leave. Patton threatened to file an emergency motion to split the spring break time and thankfully, he didn't have to. If only spring break vacation had been mentioned in their MSA. That would have alleviated almost a month of drama and child chess every year.

Thankfully, we went on our Aspen trip and had a wonderful time! The girls loved the snow, skiing, and all of the wonderful memories we created together. Emilie was so relaxed and at ease, she could just be a kid for once!

After we got back into town, we dropped Emilie off at her mother's house. We were just a mile away when Patton's cell phone rang. I saw it was Andrea before he answered. Her daughter hadn't been in the door for five minutes! She should have been hugging and kissing her little girl and asking her all the details of her ski trip! She was asking details alright, but apparently not about skiing.

Patton's responses were vague. "No, I don't know, I have no idea..." Once he hung up, I asked him for what reason she was calling. He told me that he would tell me at the house. I felt my usual adrenaline surge as I wondered what the drama du jour could possibly be.

Back at the house, Patton explained. "Emilie told her that you and I were trying to have a baby, and she wanted to know if it was true."

Her daughter was home after being away for seven days, and five minutes later, she was calling about that? So Emilie walked in the door and offered such information?

In Aspen, there *had* been perhaps a minute of baby talk. McKenna and Emilie were enjoying a bathtub filled with bubbles together and McKenna suggested in silliness, "Daddy and you should have another baby, and then the three of us could play together."

Emilie happily agreed. "Yeah, Lee-Lee, you and daddy should!" I melted every time Emilie called me that. It felt sweet and endearing.

That was the first evening of our trip. With all the exciting activities and ski stories (and no further discussion of babies), I could not imagine that Emilie would blurt that out upon walking into her mother's home.

Since this had something to do with me, I couldn't let Andrea control us, our thoughts, or our plans. I wanted to nip it in the bud to cease facilitating her power once and

39

for all. She had no right to try to deter my husband and me from conceiving a child.

When Patton went outside to get more luggage and finish unloading the car I purposefully snatched the phone from the kitchen, went into the guest bathroom on the other side of the house, and locked the door behind me.

"Andrea, this is Lisa. Patton just told me that Emilie mentioned something about us having a baby, is that right?" I asked nicely but through gritted teeth.

"Yeah, I don't know why she brought that up, but are you?" she asked, sounding deeply concerned as if it would be the worst thing we could ever do.

"Well, actually, Andrea, that is nobody's business..." I couldn't complete my sentence without her interruption.

"Yes, it is! It is too my business!" She declared.

"Andrea, Emilie has talked many times about having a baby brother or sister whether it's me or you who give it to her--" I started before she interrupted.

"I thought you guys weren't going to have children because you're too old. Forty is too old to have a child!" She exhausted my patience with that one. I was well aware that she was almost eight years my junior.

"Andrea, if and when we are pregnant and the fetus has made it past the first trimester, we will begin to announce to whomever we wish, but otherwise, it is *no* one's business." I tried to sound as calm and collected but I was seething.

"It is TOO my business!" She childishly repeated. "Get Patton on the phone; I need to speak to him!"

"No! Bye-bye, have a nice night!" I said facetiously before hanging up on her.

I exited the bathroom and filled Patton in on what had just happened. He was disappointed in me for going behind his back to call her but he agreed it wasn't her business.

Andrea called the house and Patton's cell phone several times before he finally answered her call. "Andrea, we're not trying and we're not, not trying. If it happens, great; if not, it is okay." I felt it counter-productive to listen to her opinions and give into her personal questions. But he knew if he didn't answer her, she might take her anger out on Emilie; that is all that ever mattered to him.

I told him to put her on speaker. I was livid and wanted to hear what she was saying. On speaker, echoing in our kitchen, I listened to Andrea literally sobbing in fury. "You told me you weren't going to have children with her. You told me she was too old. You are playing both of us!" She was incorrigible.

He did not like her lies and accusations. "Andrea, what are you talking about? I never said she was too old, stop lying and thinking what you wish for was true! You need counseling! I have nothing else to say to you and stop calling my house!" He hung up.

I believed he would never tell her such a thing, she was so delusional. The thought of Patton and me having a child together must have meant that she would no longer "have something that only [they] have," as she once maliciously reminded me.

She called back many times that evening, but she didn't get the last word in as she so often felt entitled. The eleventh call was the last call that we heard before turning off our phones.

The first call the next morning wasn't Andrea, but it was interesting.

Emilie (left) and McKenna enjoying the bubble bath in Aspen where the infamous "baby" conversation took place.

Submit yourselves therefore to God. Resist the devil, and he will flee from.

James 4:7

VII: Sweet Romaine

When I heard Romaine's gentle voice early the next morning, I knew something monumental must have happened.

Romaine spewed out a narrative of her most recent, and alarming, conversation with Andrea.

"I called to let you know I prayed hard for you and for your family last night and wanted to call you then, but was afraid it was too late and I might wake you up. I am so glad you gave me your phone number for the jewelry." She paused. "How are you, Lisa? Are you and the family doing okay?"

She had me concerned about what she was so prayerful and worried. I didn't want to rush her because I could tell in her almost tearful sounding voice, this was a hard call to make. I reassured her, "Oh we are doing just fine, thank you sweetie. Are you okay?"

"Well, you know Andie and I go back a few years. I have always been there for her and listened to her. I prayed for her and tried to help or just listen every time she needed to comment, complain, or just vent about Patton or you but she never seems to reciprocate when I need to vent. I have a long line of rope for our friendship but I am about at the end of it. I am tired of always hearing all the shigety about Patton and you, you know?" I told her that I understood and asked if something else was going on as she sounded truly alarming at the beginning of our call.

"Yes, I am done with Andrea, I am finished with all her games and drama! You know, she called me last night and was acting all crazy, screaming, and being all angry about it!"

42

Before I could process what "it" was, she continued. "I never told you this but Andrea confessed to me that she had keyed your car and that she's always saying how she wants to try and break up your marriage so just hearing her go on last night in such a rage about you and Patton trying to have a baby, I just had to call you! I am so worried about you both! I am so afraid she might try to hurt you!"

As frightening and upsetting as all this sounded, it wasn't surprising. I felt vindicated that I wasn't imagining or blowing out of proportion all of the concerns about Andrea that I had.

Romaine went on to say they had met at the debt collection company where they worked together a couple of years prior. Romaine said that she had often suggested that Andrea get mental health counseling but Andrea shrugged it off.

Romaine told me how Andrea had lied to her former boyfriend, Dr. Hank, and told him that she was taking birth control via an epidermal patch. "She would put it on sometimes when she was going to be intimate with him but would rip it off as soon as they were finished." I thought to myself that perhaps the good doctor found out about that and that was why Andrea came home a few days early from Las Vegas the prior Christmas.

Romaine went on to unveil the current events in Andrea's life. Andrea had been spending time with someone named Bill who Andrea found "repulsive" but he "bought her things" and she was taking advantage of that since she had no other boyfriend.

Romaine shared with me how Andrea had frequently talked about Patton physically abusing her and was now "mentally abusing" her. Andrea told Romaine that Patton was on bipolar medicine, and he never took it. She said that he never paid his child support and she was raising Emilie on her own and was "broke" all the time. Romaine said she had always felt sorry for Andrea; she believed every word of what she was told.

When Romaine finished, I shared several tidbits of information with her. I told her not only were the physical abuse allegations a lie, but they were the antithesis of the facts. I mentioned how Patton had shown me photos of the physical abuse *he* received from Andrea after only a month of marriage. There was a police report he filed but then he dropped the charges hoping she would change. I shared my own personal accounts of Andrea and her threatening words to me in front of her daughter.

I didn't know if there was a medical or psychological term for people who twisted stories to make themselves out to be the victim but I knew if there was, she had it. From what Romaine was telling me, it seemed a volte-face of the truth using her prey as the assailant and she, the victim.

Romaine was intrigued with what I shared. Her intermittent sighs and gasps spoke for themselves. She had to catch her breath before she could add that Andrea seemed to be describing herself which to Romaine began to make sense after meeting me and Patton. "You seem so happy and cheerful all the time, Andrea is always bitter and angry; she scares me!"

I extended my gratitude to Romaine for her thoughtful warning call and apologized that she was involved in so much treachery. She didn't at all blame us; she was irate with Andrea, though. "I have always tried to think of Andrea as a person who would one day finally learn from her many mistakes and change."

I agonized and searched in my mind for hope with the entire situation with Andrea for the silver lining but I feared it might never reveal itself. But God did give me a silver lining: Romaine. Romaine turned out to be a lifelong friend to me and to my family. We have continued to pray for each other and with each other. I try to keep my Andrea chat to a minimum since I know that although Andrea unintentionally brought us together, she is definitely is not what our friendship is about.

After that phone call, Romaine confronted Andrea about many of the contradictions she learned from me. Andrea denied everything and Romaine promptly ended their friendship choosing to never contact her again.

Idolatry, sorcery, enmity, strife, jealousy, fits of anger, rivalries, dissensions, divisions, envy, drunkenness, orgies, and things like these. I warn you, as I warned you before, that those who do such things will not inherit the kingdom of God.

Galatians 5:20-21

VIII: Signs and Sounds

With all that Romaine told me, I shouldn't have been surprised what Andrea's next stunt was in her strategy to make our lives a living hell.

Andrea put a "For Sale" sign in her yard the very day after the baby conversation. Patton and I assumed she wanted to make sure that when he dropped off Emilie he would see it and she would get his attention.

Of course, Patton telephoned her inquiring about the sign but she was a broken record when she went on about taking Emilie out of the Christian School that she had been attending and how she didn't want to run into me there when I took McKenna in the fall. Again, we saved her voice recording saying such in a message she left on our answering machine to use as part of the evidence intended to show her spite, alienation, and her lack of consideration for her daughter's best interest. However, the housing market was just starting to go south, so we didn't worry too much about her actually moving. Andrea was greedy and wouldn't settle for anything less than a huge profit so it was unlikely. Alas, the complaining about Patton and I having a baby and McKenna attending Emilie's school was unrelenting.

Patton got so fed up that he found it difficult to bite his tongue every time. "Andrea! I told you I am married to Lisa now! You and I will NEVER get back together. You need to move on and accept that and stop making my daughter suffer because that is not fair to her! I do not

46

want my daughter to grow up and be the selfish NOMAD that you are! Grow up and be a mother who cares about her daughter and stop trying to influence her decision on how she feels about me, Lisa, or McKenna!"

These tedious phone calls seem to be minutia in my story but the accumulation of so many and the alienating nature of several stand-out calls are worth mentioning.

Even though Emilie rarely, if ever, called Patton while she was with her mother, Patton would always remind Emilie to call her mother when she was with us. He knew from his daughter that she was being disciplined by Andrea if she didn't. This natural and nurturing gesture was simple co-parenting, even if it wasn't reciprocated.

Time after time, Patton confronted Andrea, telling her that she should never ever command Emilie to do anything from his house on his time. He explained how unfair it was to admonish, threaten or chastise Emilie for not calling twice a day when she was safe with him. He reminded Andrea that she wouldn't allow him to talk with Emilie virtually ever while she was at her house. The few times they did manage to speak, Emilie was on speaker phone. She was aloof and monotone. "Hi dad, well it is late and I have to go to bed, bye." Emilie spoke almost as if she was a robot. Patton would try to get a conversation going with her but it was evident that she felt uncomfortable. Andrea's manipulation of her daughter to denigrate was nothing short of exasperating. Years later, through Emilie (and through one of her mother's boyfriends that later lived with them) we verified that our theories of Andrea controlling, and even dictating the conversations, were accurate.

Communication was an important factor in Patton's eventual pursuit of justice. Most contact with his daughter was obstructed and controlled by Andrea. From our house, we would often hear Emilie being interrogated. It would go from "Hi mom, I am calling because you told me to so—yes…no…I'm not sure…I don't know let me ask my dad…" It was pathetic to listen to Emilie sound so automated and unloved.

If Andrea was with someone, the tone was completely different. I was curious and listened in to one or two of her calls to see if she spoke differently.

"Hey Honey! How are you doing?" Andrea said in an almost gooey tone.

"I'm fine, how are you?" Emilie would ask with genuine compassion.

"I'm good honey, are you having fun with your dad?" When Andrea was with someone, she had her charmer voice on.

"Yeah we played golf and then went out to dinner and we are about to rent a movie." Emilie said with enthusiasm.

"Oh, really who played golf?" Andrea inquired, not how did you play or good for you.

"Just me and Dad."

"Oh so just you and your dad went out for dinner?" Andrea went on.

"No, Lisa and McKenna met us at the restaurant and then we got ice cream afterwards."

"Oh, did Lisa and McKenna go and get ice cream with you and daddy?"

"No, Dad went to the grocery store to get something. Lisa took me and McKenna but we're home now." Emilie offered.

"Oh well honey, you are supposed to be spending time with daddy when you visit him. Okay, honey? Now you have your dad call me as soon as you see him, okay? You said you are going to rent a movie? Tell daddy he needs to watch that with you, and since you are visiting, you should pick out the movie. Make sure you tell him that, okay?" I hated Andrea always emphasizing that she was "visiting" when she was with us.

"Okay, but Mom, it is actually McKenna's turn to choose the movie so I am going to let her. I don't mind." Emilie said sweetly.

"Well, honey, you know you don't get much time there at your dad's so you should get to choose because McKenna lives with your father and gets to see him every day. That is nice of you to offer to let McKenna choose, but it is okay, you don't need to do that."

After this call as she often did, Emilie sprang up from her chair, racing to her father to give him the phone. "Dad, here, you need to call my mom!"

"Okay, honey, let me empty these bags and go to the bathroom then I will." Emilie was insistent that he call Andrea.

"No, Dad, call her now!" Emilie urgently ordered.

"Honey, relax. I will call her after I use the restroom." Patton attempted to soothe her.

"Dad, I don't want to get in trouble because you didn't call her back. She will spank me or make me go to bed early!" Emilie justified.

When Patton got on the phone with Andrea, he anticipated the usual instructions and admonitions.

"Hey, Emilie told me you weren't around this morning when she woke up and that she had to hang out with Lisa and McKenna?" Andrea barreled out.

Patton attempted to answer, "Right, I left at six-thirty for my seven--"

"Patton, you are supposed to be spending time with your daughter, not Lisa! You are her parent. You and Emilie should be spending quality time together. That is what she wants. She doesn't even like spending time with Lisa or McKenna!"

I would have slammed the phone down if someone talked about my husband like that. But Patton, ever the peacekeeper felt the need to placate her, again, so she wouldn't reprimand Emilie. "That's not true, Andrea. That might be what you want to believe, but it isn't true; they do a girls' day every once in a while and Emilie always appreciates it and has fun with them. I got back by eleven-thirty this morning and Emilie slept in until almost ten so I didn't lose much time with her. You don't spend

49

every waking moment doing things with Emilie, Andrea so don't--"

"Well, I don't have time to fix your and Emilie's relationship. That is between you two, but I know she doesn't like spending any of her time with Lisa." Per usual, Andrea hung up as soon as she interrupted his logic and got that infamous last insulting word in.

Patton always said, "you can't reason with an unreasonable person." He added the conversation to our documentation.

A couple of weeks later, Patton was up in the attic when Andrea called. She sounded shocked to hear my voice. I had just gotten back into town that morning and I suppose she thought I was still away. Once she realized that I was home, she rescinded her offer to let Patton have some extra time with Emilie that she presented him a few hours prior.

"Oh, Patton, I thought it was just going to be you and Emilie; never mind." We had dated for two years and been married for three years at that point; she was never going to accept our marriage.

Then there were the calls of power, "Hey, Emilie just told me you were going to ..." If it sounded like fun, Andrea would come up with a reason that Patton shouldn't do it. For example if Emilie told her mother that we were going to Patton's family lake house, her mother would tell Patton that she couldn't go in the lake because lakes were "dirty and dangerous." Naturally, Emilie would later mimic those sentiments. Fortunately, Emilie was still young enough to embrace her father's love and guidance and would often eventually release her mother's negative influence about her dad after spending quality time with him.

There were standard boundaries though that Emilie was instructed to follow when she was with us. Andrea told Emilie that she wasn't allowed to take aspirin, Tylenol, or any medicines at our house, nor was Patton "allowed to" take Emilie to the doctor, hospital, or even

50

for a haircut! At almost seven years old, this child wasn't the happy and fun-loving young lady she once was, she was her mother's prisoner, her minion, her pawn and her meal ticket. I believed this emotional abuse had to have long-term repercussions on Emilie and it never stopped worrying me. From the time Emilie was six years old, I urged Patton to get his daughter into counseling numerous times, but he refused. "In our MSA, it says, 'the parents shall contact each other if Emilie ever gets medical attention.' If I take her to a counselor, her mother will go and lie about me and my relationship with my daughter. Then my daughter suffers wondering why she needs mental health counseling."

I didn't get it. It seemed to me the counselors could figure that out. At least they would be privy to the obvious alienation and later serve as possible witnesses at the custody hearing.

I contemplated leaving my marriage because I felt like we would never be able to escape Andrea's irrationality and that I had no say in parenting, rather step-parenting Emilie. I had to listen to and live through all the grief and lies while trying to accept and excuse Emilie's increasingly bad behavior and insolence she was gleaning from her mother. Emilie began to backtalk, pinch Patton's arms, flick her fingers at him, and shove him when she didn't like him telling her to do homework, for example. I wondered if Emilie would ever be able to change or shrug off her mother's demands and alienation or if would she grow up to be just like her.

All of it hit home when Emilie told Patton that her mom didn't like it when Emilie and her dad hugged at drop off time, "My mom said 'it takes too much time and it looks like we are trying to make her jealous.'" Emilie would literally hug or kiss us goodbye blocks before we got to her house so her mom wouldn't see her being so affectionate toward us. It was beyond sad, it was emotional abuse.

As much as it was difficult for me to watch my stepdaughter be so tormented and controlled, it was clearly more so for Patton. He looked almost depressed at each drop off, not for himself, but for his daughter's rigid regulations set by her mother. We talked about how Emilie needed to witness a normal family, normal relationships, and normal behaviors. I worked to reduce my stress and made it a challenge to not get bothered or personally offended. I prayed that Emilie would mature quickly so that she could see through her mother and realize that she was using her, controlling her, and even making her own life less fulfilling by limiting her boundaries when she spent time with us or our extended family.

When Patton's parents drove for four hours to attend the one hour celebration of Grandparents' Day at Emilie's school, for example, Andrea purposely preplanned a play date directly after school so that she could keep Emilie from Patton and his parents. She hurried her down the stairs at school, the moment it was over. When I learned this, I called the mother of the play date. She told me that Andrea had called her that morning, begging her to watch Emilie after Grandparent's Day. Our hearts bled for Emilie.

Vacationing at Universal Studios, Orlando, FL.

Refrain from anger, and forsake wrath! Fret not yourself;
it tends only to evil.
   Psalm 37:8

IX: Ready, Set, Go…

   Finally the legal battle was about to truly commence. Andrea was served Patton's motion to modify custody the Friday prior to Valentine's Day, 2007. The light at the end of the tunnel seemed like an actual possibility after all! If Patton won his case, not only would Emilie be a winner but he and I could finally put an end to the obsessive amount of time we were devoting to Emilie's angst and mental torture. Perhaps we could once again become passionate about our marriage!

   I was losing myself. The priorities in our two-year marriage had become: Emilie, Andrea (and her wrath), Patton's work and legal endeavors for Emilie, me, McKenna, and finally, our marriage. It was surreal that McKenna and I had any sense of value at all by this time.

   My daughter never grew really close to Patton. She said she "never felt important" to him. I reminded her that he was providing a wonderful life for her. And as a stay-at-home mom, I was able to make up for his minimal time with her. I didn't really know how to mend fences when she became detached from him, but I tried, over and over, to help her feel confidence in his love for her.

   This, too, may have been Andrea's work. She clearly wanted McKenna, who had never known her own biological father, to feel like an outsider with Patton. If McKenna answered the phone, Andrea would ask with distain. "Can I speak with Emilie's father?" Andrea was well aware that McKenna called Patton her daddy.

   Emilie often repeated that Patton was her real dad and that McKenna didn't have a real dad because her dad "never met her."

McKenna, ever confident, even as an eight-year-old retorted that she knew Patton was her stepdad. "Daddy said that he is my dad, too. That isn't nice for your mother to say that!"

The day Andrea was served with the custody petition, she called Patton yelling and suggesting that he was trying to get out of paying child support! She wasn't a very logical person. If so, she would have understood that if he was trying to get out of child support, he would not be spending an exorbitant amount of money fighting for more time with his daughter. (The custody battle ultimately cost him more than $100,000.)

Andrea no longer had friends, to my knowledge, who could buffer the situation and remove some of her wrath. For Patton this meant things got even worse. She would not answer the phone at all when he called to speak with his daughter and kept that "For Sale" sign posted in front of her house. On several occasions, she withheld his legal visitation. Although Patton presented this at various hearings, her contempt went unpunished, thus enabling further alienating behavior by Andrea. She got away with each and every alienation tactic.

Patton was much more cautious. He never expressed any of his true opinions or divulged any of Andrea's lies and threats to his daughter. I thought his daughter needed to know the truth about her mother. Emilie should know that what Andrea was doing was wrong and unkind. Patton disagreed, and was right in saying that it wasn't right to put Emilie in the middle especially since her mother was already doing that.

Andrea began hanging up the phone on Patton and even her daughter, if either asked if Emilie could stay overnight rather than return home at eight o'clock per the "minimum visitation" guideline in the MSA.

At drop offs at a location that Andrea suddenly unilaterally decided—a police station parking lot, that later changed to a bank parking lot—Andrea waited in her car, on her phone and never made eye contact with any of us.

When Emilie got in the car, she didn't hang up her phone or acknowledge this poor little girl. If my husband had any questions or comments for Andrea about school, homework, health, sports, or any concern, she would keep that phone glued to her ear and act like she couldn't hear him. Then she would speed off aimlessly through the parking lot.

Pretty much anything that my husband needed to say or ask of Andrea was out of the question. Patton was unable to obtain Emilie's baby photos, a copy of her birth certificate, her social security number, or Andrea's consent to obtain a passport for Emilie. It seemed the only connection she cared for regarding his paternal rights was him paying her child support.

Patton ultimately had to get his daughter's social security number by going into the school office and checking her records there. That experience was not just embarrassing, it was humiliating. Thankfully her school had already seen Andrea's hostile behavior on campus several times.

The custody trial couldn't come soon enough! But the process of litigation, hearings, mediations, and numerous continuances meant it would be more than two years before the case went to trial in August, 2009.

I am not the most patient person so awaiting the trial was biting at me. I wanted to confront Andrea many times and tell her that I was privy to all those nasty character defamations she told other people about my husband needing medication because he was bipolar and her lies about him cheating on her with me causing their marriage to end. I wanted to share that taking her healthy daughter to the doctor's office twenty-five times in less than eighteen months, didn't make her Mother of the Year, it put up red flags that would be noticed by any judge or psychologist. I wanted to call her out about everything and I wanted her to know that Patton and I both knew of all of her sneaky and manipulating ways! How I wished that I could share with Andrea that my husband only played nice with her for the possibility of more time with Emilie and to alleviate his daughter's stress, not because he thought kindly of her. I wanted to say that telling a child that their father didn't care about or love them was not only manipulative but it was emotionally abusive! But I followed my husband's altruistic lead and kept my mouth shut.

As the trial approached, my marriage grew tenser. I was starting to build resentment for Patton as I still saw him as being naïve and an enabler. Then I realized that Andrea was making an indirect pawn out of me and I would not permit that.

Andrea was someone who would continue to be present in my life until Emilie went to college so I prayed for strength, guidance, and change. God answered by granting me forgiveness and compassion toward Andrea, even pushing me to offer several more olive branches over the years. Although she wore me down, I still tried to do what He wanted me to do. For example on Mother's Day, Christmas, and even her birthday, I took cute photos of Emilie, created a collage and purchased a pretty frame to put them in. Patton sometimes allowed Emilie to pick out a small piece of jewelry for her mom. Emilie would be excited to present her wrapped gift but Emilie later told us that her mom "didn't wear" or "didn't like" what she got and "took it back" or "put it away to wear another time."

When McKenna began attending the same school that Emilie did, I felt comfortable enough to help out in my daughter's classroom on a regular basis. In fact, I began volunteering for other needs the school had, like manning the front office while in the staff was in meetings, or simply making copies for teachers. My volunteering soon became fairly regular, so much in that I was named the school's first Volunteer of the Year.

I was even asked to apply as a substitute teacher. I did, and was hired. I felt surrounded by this amazing Christian staff, one person kinder than the next.

I was afraid it wouldn't be too long before Andrea found out. But I resolved that she was not going to dictate my life. Still, I hoped it would go smoothly.

Sooner than I expected, Andrea came in with widened eyes and gritted teeth asking me what I was doing there at the school. I told her that I filled in at the front desk for staff meetings.

"May I help you with something?" I asked trying to break her gaze.

She had nothing to say; she just stood there. I decided to go to the small adjacent copier room to let her know she hadn't fazed me. I didn't want to let her know that I was petrified of her. In any case, I felt sure she wouldn't cause a scene at the school. I was wrong.

"Lisa! I am talking to you!" she barked, as if I was her seven-year-old daughter.

At the copier, I felt a small sense of satisfaction as I was sure that the office staff could see and hear her demand. When I went back to my post and casually sat down, I looked up to her and confidently reiterated my purpose for being there. Her pupils ballooned in rage. She demanded to speak with the principal, Dr. Planter.

Dr. Planter was in her late fifties and had one of the kindest Christian hearts imaginable. I could almost see a halo over her head as I am sure to this day she is one of God's most prized angels walking the earth.

I buzzed into Marianne, Dr. Planter's secretary, to ask for an immediate conference per Andrea's request. I didn't mind facilitating the meeting; I'd hoped she would have one, actually. Andrea would dig her own grave complaining about her husband's wife.

Unfortunately, Dr. Planter wasn't available but that didn't stop Andrea. Uninvited, and with her usual sense of entitlement, she waltzed right back into Marianne's office and slammed the door shut!

A few days later, Patton and I were called by Dr. Planter to schedule a conference. My husband appeared telephonically since his work precluded him from attending but I was present in her office for the meeting. Dr. Planter had no intention of reprimanding Patton and me for what she heard from Andrea but rather to advise us of the concerns that the school had with *Andrea*! Dr. Planter had taken two pages of notes during her meeting with Andrea. (See Ch.9 Figs.2 & 3) These were also duplicated for Emilie's school file.

[REDACTED]   Mtg. 12:00 - 1:05   2-26-09

[REDACTED] [father?] present for the entire mtg; I called Karen to convene about 12:40.

b. [REDACTED] trying to get custody of [REDACTED] w/ withholding child support

1. [REDACTED] has developed a facial tic, due to stress (crying)

2. He has her 2 hrs on M+W & everyother weekend.

3. He's going to try to take [REDACTED] a ski trip

4. [REDACTED] is trying to get her first a lifestyle

5. " If you want to call your "Mom," you can

6. She talked w/ [REDACTED] her [REDACTED] is stomach aches

c. Things at SOES she wants is concerned about:

1. [REDACTED] has brought "Happy Meals" to [REDACTED] at SOES   *Not necessary
   when [REDACTED] has packed a lunch / or has brought cookies [for her]   or appropriate

2. She didn't get a school directory (the ones diff copy were mailed).
   I'll give her another one.

3. A mom who spends time w/ him who spends time w/ me seems to be
   talking to others about th [REDACTED]
   Lisa + [REDACTED]'s mom are good friends.

d. Karen - Kindergarten have treated the staff was rude & demanding.
   You were very demanding when you called to
   me, Suzanne, Sandi, Cheri

[REDACTED]

E. "Lisa told her "I'm employed here." It's a conflict of interest to hire her.

E. Karen presented the question of whether [REDACTED] should be here
   that it would be easier for [REDACTED] to have her in an
   environment that wouldn't [REDACTED] conflicts with [REDACTED] + Lisa
   [REDACTED] agreed + said she'd thought of that. I gave her a [REDACTED]

Re-enrollment Considerations

Parent:
Student: ██████████████████████   Date: _2-26-07_

Teacher: ██████████████████████   Grade _1_

Problems that may prevent student's acceptance for next school year:

1. _Mother's demands to change a situation immediately_

2. _Mother's demand to not allow ████ 's stepmother in her room_

3. _Mother's demand that a child be removed from ████ 's class_

4. _the following day_

5. _Mother's demands on our Office Staff_

Improvements that need to be made by May 1 to be considered for enrollment for August:

1. _Mother's kind interactions with SCS personnel_

2. _Mother's support of school policy_

3. _Mother's use of "chain of command" on policy matters_

4. _____

5. _____

Presented to ████ at a face-to-face conference in my office on 2/26/07.

██████████████

(Ch.9 Fig.3)

60

Interestingly enough, on the Re-enrollment Consideration form, the word "Student" was crossed out and written in was the word "Parent". It seemed every bit of concern about Emilie re-enrolling for the school the following year was due to Andrea, not at all Emilie. Once again, Andrea's actions had impacted Emilie's best interest.

Dr. Planter's penmanship, while beautiful and elegant, was also a bit difficult to decipher. In short, Andrea expressed several defamations and character slurs about us to Dr. Planter. She started with, "Patton is trying to get custody and is *withholding* his child support!" She continued in a ramble, apparently.

"He only sees Emilie for two hours on Mondays and Wednesdays and every other weekend" and "He is going to try to take Emilie on a ski trip!" Andrea also accused my husband of causing Emilie's new facial tics and stomach aches.

About me, Andrea shared that, "Lisa is trying to get me fired from my job" and expressed that she felt it was "unnecessary and inappropriate" that I "brought cookies into Emilie's class." Andrea told Dr. Planter that if I "wanted her to, Emilie was allowed to call me mom." Andrea also condemned my working at the school, saying that she felt it was "a conflict of interest." Finally she said that, "A mom that spends time with Lisa, seems to be talking about me."

Whew, that was a lot to get off her chest! Especially important to mention that I brought a Happy Meal in to Emilie *once* for lunch. She also twisted Patton's visitation time to only two hours on Mondays and Wednesdays when at the time it was actually five hours each on those days.

Andrea demanded "immediate change." She wanted me to be fired and never allowed into Emilie's classroom again. Andrea wanted Patton to be barred from campus. She told Emilie's teachers and other staff members that he was "forbidden" to be there and that she was the "primary custodial parent."

61

Finally, Andrea wanted a child that allegedly victimized Emilie on the ladder of a slide in a playground, removed from the school immediately.

The school did take action on the latter following the proper protocol. However, that wasn't soon enough for Andrea, who called the police on the young student who supposedly pulled Emilie's skort down while she was ahead of him on the ladder of a slide. The police investigated the child, Emilie, and the supervising teachers.

This conference with Dr. Planter, and the apprehension of the school continuing to allow Emilie to attend because of her mother's actions would serve as just a fraction of the evidence in Emilie's school file that substantiated the impact of Andrea's wrath and alienation.

Over the speakerphone, my husband responded to Andrea's financial accusations telling Dr. Planter that he had never been more than one week late on his child support and that he also always paid for 100 percent of all school tuition and expenses. He offered to provide records of each and every support payment from the Florida Department of Revenue. By the following week, he had. Patton had paid more payments early than he did late but most were exactly on time. It wasn't because Dr. Planter didn't trust him, she did, but my husband wanted his daughter's school to know that Andrea was spreading false and disparaging comments about him; this was expressly prohibited in their MSA.

When Patton finished speaking, I took a few minutes and summarized the first week of school during which Andrea showed up and refused to relinquish Emilie's backpack to me when it was our pick up day. I told Dr. Planter I had hoped that the incident wasn't indicative of what would happen that school year but that I knew reasonably from her track record, it would. I explained how on that day my stepdaughter's face looked lost and torn as her eyes dodged from her mother, to me, and back to her mother for her final decision. I felt so sorry for her.

Andrea didn't seem to mind the audience of parents and students filling the classroom threshold where the incident took place. In fact, she seemed to have no worry at all. It was as if she was void of any semblance of a conscience.

Regarding the facial tics, I couldn't believe that Andrea was trying to tell Emilie's principal that they were a result of "Patton causing stress" to his daughter. How offensive especially considering that I listened far too often to Emilie sharing how her mother would spank and slap her. Andrea neglected to tell Dr. Planter she punished Emilie physically and constantly undermined and denigrated Patton as Emilie's father.

I shared with Dr. Planter, Emilie's new-found anger, resentment, and sadness which was symptomatic of parental alienation. I told the principal that Emilie frequently divulged how she was scolded by her mother if she disclosed a single thing about her mother's home, life, or any person associated with them. That was actually fine, we didn't want details or any information for it gave Patton more to worry about.

But it had gotten to the point that if we asked how Emilie how her weekend was or how she was feeling (if she had been ill) Emilie consistently answered, "I don't know, you have to ask my mom." She was loyal to her abuser.

Dr. Planter seemed to completely understand and welcome the information we provided to refute Andrea's poor impulse control and lies. She told us specifically that as long as we were going to be a part of Emilie's schooling and Andrea would not try to involve the school or Emilie's teacher in her personal matters, they would allow Emilie to continue.

As Emilie got older though, she appeared to sometimes emulate her mother by playing the victim as she began to blame others for occasional shortcomings at school. For example, she would suggest that a teacher "didn't teach it" if she did poorly on an assignment or test. Her teachers refuted that by telling us the information was being taught

63

in class, and several students were achieving high marks. Perhaps Emilie couldn't concentrate since her mother had completely stressed her out.

If school wasn't the most pressing issue in Emilie's life, socializing with her peers, was inching its way to the top. Patton and I were social people; we enjoyed entertaining in our home or spending time with friends. McKenna, was also a very outgoing young lady with a close circle of friends upward of forty children, girls and boys, and had fairly regular parties at our house. Like most children her age, McKenna delighted in outings to the club pool, theme parks, movies, the mall, sleepovers, bowling, and a variety of other venues. To her social life, McKenna added modeling, cotillion, piano, Girl Scouts, Christian Youth Group, triathlons, and swim team. She was always busy.

By contrast, Emilie participated in many sports but sadly had only a friend or two. Andrea was extremely anti-social so we were concerned that this might be a limitation she passed down to her daughter. One parent openly admitted that they had been alarmed by the promiscuous clothing Andrea wore that exposed her cleavage and buttock cheeks when she dropped off or picked up Emilie from school. Once they met Patton and me, they allowed their child to visit Emilie but only while she was at our home.

McKenna, who had very little in common with Emilie, would pitch in to help boost Emilie's self-esteem on occasion. McKenna would give Emilie "makeovers" and sometime share her friends when they came over.

As I have seen, those who plow iniquity and sow trouble reap the same.
  Job 4:8

X: At the Starting Gate

Patton's motion to modify visitation/time-sharing was solely for 'the best interest" of his daughter which is what the law required him to prove. Patton needed to reduce Andrea's influence on their daughter which would also facilitate more exposure to some semblance of normalcy and stability, from us.

The first emergency motion for hearing that Patton filed was for his brother's wedding, and after school pick-up time to be restored to what he had been enjoying for the first three years of Emilie's education. Looking to frustrate Patton, Andrea looked for loopholes in their MSA and used it punitively. Andrea had always let Patton pick Emilie up from school on his visitation days. However, the MSA actually said Patton was entitled to "at a minimum from 5pm to 8pm" on the agreement. It seemed obvious that my marriage to Patton pushed her to eliminate his more liberal time with his daughter so no longer was Patton able to pick his daughter up from school. Only the courts could change this.

About the same age as my husband, Judge A was a man of few words. He seemed to want to move things along without too much detail. When Andrea spoke out of turn with random lies and nebulous gibberish, he commanded her to, "Be quiet!" and "Wait until I ask for you to speak!"

The judge granted my husband's motion to restore the status quo; after school pick-up time of three o'clock would resume.

65

Andrea attempted to change his ruling by interrupting him again. "But my daughter and I have a routine after school and she wants to do her homework with me!"

The Judge looked at her sternly. "Ma'am, what routine do you and your daughter have after school that must continue every Monday and Wednesday?"

She was silent for just a beat and then stammered "Well, we like to read."

"Well, then you may continue to read to your daughter every night at bedtime or at eight o'clock when you get her back to your house."

Andrea was so acclimated to getting what she wanted she could hardly contain herself. She was very flush in color and her hands seemed to be those of a person with Parkinson's disease, uncontrollably shaky. I couldn't help but feel internally gleeful that someone finally reprimanded Andrea.

Judge A wasn't finished.

His honor, in closing of that motion, asked if there were any other issues regarding this matter. My husband saw a window to ask the judge to please allow me, his wife, to pick up Emilie from school on occasion if he was running tardy or in court for a trial. Andrea had gone on a frenzy of removing my name from all school records pertaining to Emilie including the pick-up list and names of emergency contacts.

"Mr. Young, as long as you trust the individual and they don't have a sexual predator or offender background, then you may choose whoever you would like to pick her up from school on your visitation days. Miss Young, you are able to do the very same thing. Now is that acceptable to everyone?"

Against her counsel's warning, Andrea could not contain herself. "I don't think that is fair. It is Patton's visitation and not his wife's." The Judge just shook his head as if he had enough of her, disregarded her, and ordered the motion he said prior to her outburst.

66

The final motion for the hearing was about Patton's brother getting married in Boston. Emilie and McKenna were asked to be the flower girls; what an honor! The girls were very excited for the plane ride and the rose petal duty. Although Patton asked Andrea two months in advance if he could switch weekends with her so that Emilie could go to Boston, Andrea wouldn't budge as if she wanted Emilie's life to be once again unfulfilling and non-joyful. Anything that Patton wanted, she refused. She used Emilie as a pawn and the judge must have agreed as he again, ruled in my husband's favor and also ordered that Andrea would be paying the court fees for that emergency hearing as she should have granted Patton the right to allow him to take Emilie to Boston.

After the hearing, Patton and I talked about how Andrea despised losing. We anticipated that she would do her utmost to make Patton and Emilie's relationship even more miserable. She did.

A couple of months later, Andrea filed a counterclaim to increase her child support. She knew that Patton had had one exceptional earnings year and thought she deserved more money. Patton didn't want to have to pay accountants and legal fees so he enlisted the help of a family law friend to compute the amount to which she was entitled and found that year, since he had earned double what he usually earned, Andrea would be entitled to about $300 more each month. Florida law uses the last three years average earnings to calculate the amount. Without the State of Florida or courts intervening, Patton began paying the additional amount. No one could deny my husband's integrity.

Our expenses were mounting. Our lifestyle, savings, renovations and dreams were put on the back burner, along with our marriage. Patton not only had to pay his own legal costs and fees but for Andrea's also, since she showed an inability to pay? Andrea's "temporary attorney's fees and costs" were later ordered by Judge B, who took the case when Judge A moved from civil court to criminal court.

I am not sure why Judge B thought Andrea was more destitute or needy than my husband. With all of my husband's personal loans and debts, it simply couldn't be true. We knew of her finances and her spending habits. Andrea was a miser. According to Emilie, she and her mom would shop for clothing at Goodwill or Salvation Army. They went to buffets and ordered just one meal which they shared. If they got caught they wouldn't return. Andrea saved every penny and rarely indulged in anything remotely extravagant, except her car which was either a Mercedes or a BMW. Andrea even managed to invest in a little cabin an hour north of us and a small ranch home, both of which brought in rental income. While her employment wages hovered around $10,000 a year, her assets proved she certainly wasn't the struggling single mother she painted herself to be. She clearly used Patton's support and initial divorce settlement, wisely. We learned from financial disclosure, that the $178,000 check she received in settlement for the divorce was still two-thirds intact in a savings account.

But Andrea wasn't nearly so careful with Patton's funds. She found ways to deplete his bank account – legally.

For every email sent to and reviewed by Andrea's attorney, a quarter-hour was billed. Since Andrea was awarded attorney's fees and her attorney considered this case to be "highly contentious" he charged $400 an hour, she wasted no time taking advantage of this. At $100 per email, Patton's expenses were skyrocketing quickly! Andrea sometimes emailed her attorney three or four times in one day! We prayed that all this money spent would be worth it in the long run and would result in Emilie's favor to be with a stable, loving father and his family.

*Let the wise hear and increase in learning, and the one
who understands obtain guidance*
    Proverbs 1:5

XI: Researching Crazy

Once the legal battle was well into the first phase, I
began organizing the detailed documentation, audio files,
videos, photos, and paperwork we would be using as
evidence against Andrea.   The accumulation of so much
information put my curiosity into overdrive. I went into a
research frenzy!

I wondered about the doctor who would soon be doing
the custody evaluation. Would he see through Andrea's
sneaky veneer or would she get away with everything as
she generally did?

I wanted to understand Andrea's mental-scape.   I
started my mission by typing relevant search terms on the
Internet.   When I typed in "alienation, manipulation of
children, impulse control, rage, lying..." I noticed the
same types of articles appearing repeatedly. The traits and
actions I had witnessed from Andrea seemed to be
symptomatic of several different psychological disorders,
including Borderline Personality Disorder, Narcissistic
Personality Disorder (NPD), Bipolar Disorder, and the big
one, Psychopathy. Patton later shared with me that Andrea
had once been diagnosed with Narcissistic Personality
Disorder but she didn't agree or follow through with any
treatment.

I knew virtually nothing about any of those disorders
and decided to educate myself. I continued my on-line
research and delved into at least a half-dozen books from
the library and the bookstore. The more I gleaned, the
more I became intrigued and almost obsessed with
learning more.   Maybe I should have studied psychology

instead of computer science, I thought. It was fascinating to learn about the human mind.

I familiarized myself with the term, "parental alienation." Parental Alienation Syndrome, was coined in the 1980's by forensic psychiatrist, Dr. Richard Gardner, M.D. He stated that children can be brainwashed by the custodial parent to develop an irrational hatred for the other parent.[1]

Andrea definitely denigrated, criticized, attacked, manipulated, controlled and attempted to eliminate any normal relationship Emilie and Patton could have together. With all of those earmarks, parental alienation syndrome was substantially obvious.

The syndrome is still questionable in the medical and legal fields with some even referring to it as "junk science." However, when you personally witness and live through so many corroborating incidents, it is anything but. Clearly, we were not alone. Dr. Gardner's vast studies included many people who experienced the abusive nature of the syndrome. He also found that women were responsible for ninety-percent of the serious alienation cases. [2]

I, myself, had joined several on-line support groups including "Second Wives Club" and "Parental Alienation Worldwide Support Group" on Facebook. How quickly I learned this was such an epidemic that truly required family law reform in every county of every state.

The books I read about parental alienation were mostly clinical and offered the same advice which was exactly what Patton had already been doing for years; be kind, don't say anything bad about the other parent and don't let the child know there is any issue. But following those rules seemed to be getting him nowhere with Andrea.

Parental alienation seemed to be more of an effect of a personality disorder, not an actual diagnosis that was legally or medically accepted. I wanted to get to the core, to the root of the problem.

Andrea was estranged from her parents. When she did have relationship with them, she admitted that she always hated her mother and that she was instead, a "daddy's girl." In fact, I recall early in our courtship, Andrea telling Patton that her mother had been diagnosed with cancer. This turned out to be untrue, yet Andrea continued to use her mother's declining health malevolently as a ploy to incite Patton's pity and affection for her.

Like myself, Andrea grew up in Maryland before settling in Florida. Her parents migrated to a city in Florida just a half-hour away from our residence. Her father was a retired police officer and her mother, worked at a college as an executive assistant. Andrea had only one sibling and he was a doctor living in Louisiana.

My mind raced as I dissected Andrea and her potential underlying symptoms and causes of her behaviors. She had admitted to being diagnosed with bulimia and anorexia as a teen. Patton and I already knew first hand that Andrea was a compulsive liar, violent, and sadistic. Andrea was also anti-social.

When Patton and Andrea were married, they sought counseling as an attempt to salvage their relationship. This was when the psychologist, Dr. R., told them that Andrea appeared to have NPD, and prescribed therapy, but Andrea was in denial and didn't comply. This somehow later manifested itself into Andrea telling people that Patton had "bipolar disorder" and "he refused to take his medication," according to what Romaine and others shared with us.

Through my studies and investigation, I learned that narcissism was in a sense, a lesser form of psychopathy. A person with narcissism lacked empathy, disregarded the rules of life, and seemed to be impulsively evil and manipulative. Psychopaths had all of those traits but were more calculated in their manipulations and more sadistic in that they enjoyed seeing pain in their prey (even sometimes finding it humorous). They also seemed to not be able, or chose not to, control their impulses. I wondered if Andrea could be a psychopath.

From my research, I learned that many psychopaths were not killers as my ignorance led me to believe. Many were everyday people who managed to function in society with jobs and families. They had a dark side that was concealed behind a false charm when they needed to shield themselves. They had the ultimate disguise as loving and caring people because they conformed to society's norm.

This was terrifying to read. I learned that psychopaths didn't truly feel emotions, but they did know what was expected of them.

A psychopath never feels love. A psychopath only says they do because it is what society expects and it is a way that they use "love" as a vehicle to get something they want. [3]

This was one of the most frightening illnesses imaginable and prior to reading *Without Conscience, The Disturbing World of the Psychopaths among Us* by Dr. Robert D. Hare, PhD, I was oblivious to the real definition and characteristics of this mental illness.

While I read, I was hoping that the judges, mediators, custody evaluators, and parent coordinators were well-versed on psychopathy and other related mental disorders especially since psychopathy is incurable.

It is imperative, as Dr. Hare reminded me in his book, that the psychopathy checklist he supplied be used as a clinical tool for professional use only. The truth is when I looked at Hare's *Key Symptoms of Psychopathy*[4] I could honestly place check marks next to each and every symptom in relation to her. (See next page)

Emotional/Interpersonal	*Social Deviance*
• Glib and Superficial√	• Impulsive√
• Egocentric and Grandiose√	• Poor Behavior Controls√
• Lack of Remorse or guilt√	• Need For Excitement√
• Lack of Empathy√	• Lack of Responsibly√
• Deceitful and Manipulative√	• Early Behavioral Problems√
• Shallow emotions√	• Adult Antisocial Behavior√

Analyzing the traits that Dr. Hare listed made me feel uncomfortable. I wondered how this innocent child could possibly feel living at her mother's house more than 80% of the time.

Emilie gradually developed an embittered and disrespectful attitude and new physiological traits: fidgeting, less focus, and very rapid, random eye blinking (twitches). These symptomatic anxiety reactions tended to increase the hours nearing the time she was due to go back to her mother's house after her visitation with us.

This book about psychopathy made far too much sense to me. I was convinced more than ever that Andrea needed psychological help before something truly tragic happened to Emilie.

When the righteous cry for help, the Lord hears and delivers them out of all their troubles. The Lord is near to the brokenhearted and saves the crushed in spirit. Many are the afflictions of the righteous, but the Lord delivers him out of them all. He keeps all his bones; not one of them is broken.
Psalm 34:17-20

XII: Custody Evaluation

In Florida, when issues of visitation, parental responsibility, or residential placement of the child is in controversy, the court may appoint "an expert" for an evaluation. The American Psychological Association Guideline for custody evaluation reads: "Psychologists strive to employ multiple methods of data gathering." The guideline further states: "Psychologists strive to employ optimally diverse and accurate methods for addressing the questions raised in a specific child custody evaluation. Direct methods of data gathering typically include such components as psychological testing, clinical interview and behavioral observation. Psychologists may also have documentation from a variety of sources (e.g., schools, health care providers, child-care providers, agencies and other institutions) and frequently make contact with extended family, friends, and acquaintances, and other collateral sources when the resulting information is likely to be relevant. Psychologists may seek corroboration of information gathered from third parties and are encouraged to document the bases of their eventual conclusion." [5]

In Patton and Andrea's case, the person to help determine custody modification to be in the best interest of the child was Dr. Boot. Per Dr. Boot's report, he did *not* meet with anyone else for collateral information or observations. This was a huge disappointment and could completely shut down the opportunity for Patton to be

74

granted additional time with Emilie if Judge B relied primarily on his evaluation. Had the doctor met with anyone at all from Emilie's school, he would have corroboratory evidence supporting the countless lies and manipulations by Andrea. Emilie was in third grade already so he could have met with any of her four teachers (including kindergarten) or with the principal of the school, the after-care supervisors or even the secretaries in the front office. He didn't.

As we later learned, Dr. Boot had considered other collateral material in his report—impartially provided by Andrea! We were told to provide three character letters for Dr. Boot but that was all, nothing more. Andrea brought a dozen! Most, if not all, were past dated from people who weren't even a part of her life anymore, including her parents.

Of the collateral letters submitted ex parté from Andrea, one was from the Safe Start Program indicating that Andrea and Emilie were victims of domestic violence. It is terrifying that anyone can go to a place such as this and claim domestic violence. Apparently Safe Start also does not evaluate such claims and never made an effort to verify such defamations. The reality was that *Patton* was the abused spouse, not Andrea. Had Patton had any knowledge of Andrea taking their daughter anywhere for the sole purpose of gaining a false affirmation, he would have produced the pictures of his bloodied fat lip and scarred face from where Andrea socked him in one of her many rages. It was unfair that Patton was unaware of this defamatory information. He wasn't privy to any of these collateral pieces from Andrea until just before trial when Patton received the discovery from Andrea's attorneys, long after Dr. Boot submitted his final recommendation.

Finally, in his report he listed several pages of "incidents of hostile and aggressive behaviors by Patton toward Andrea and Emilie," purely unsubstantiated and biased based only on Andrea's self-serving hand written fictitious journals. Andrea was delusional but she knew

75

how to "charm" men, clearly, she had done just that to Dr. Boot. Again, if Dr. Boot was to consider ex parte information, we could have printed extensive documentation, threats on audio, and various other pieces of evidence to submit for his consideration.

Florida was the first of only two states in the US at the time with an immunity law for court-appointed psychologists performing custody evaluations; they were protected from lawsuits. It didn't surprise me that nearly eighty-percent of all complaints filed to the Florida Board of Psychology were for custody evaluations.[6]

Dr. Boot did administer the MMPI-2, the MCMI-III, the PAI, and the BASC-II tests to Patton and Andrea as well as the clinical observations and parenting stress inventory assessment. However those personal interviews he could have had, but didn't, with coaches, neighbors, and employers would have revealed the truth about Andrea and how she lied throughout much if not all of her interviews with him.

For example, some of Andrea's statements Dr. Boot mentioned in his report were: "he lied a lot about where he was, he would get angry and break things, he threw things at [her] head while she was pregnant, he used to not show up or call for his scheduled visitation, now he doesn't miss any and thinks he is father of the year."

Andrea stated that she had two years of college education and that she had never been fired from a job. Andrea didn't have one year of college, never mind, two. She was fired from all of the four part-time jobs she held since I had known her. She also mentioned how she was newly employed at an architectural firm doing filing. She neglected to say that it was her boyfriend at the time, Dave's home-based sole proprietorship. We're not even sure she ever worked there as there was no evidence nor claim of it in her tax records. Andrea also denied any psychiatric hospitalization when she was a teen although she did admit to some counseling for anorexia/bulimia. He parents actually had her committed for her eating

76

disorder and counseling. Andrea told Patton while they were courting that is why she loathed her mother because she blamed her for "tricking her" when she was committed/hospitalized. She also denied ever being arrested. Patton's best friend, Jim, had been her attorney for a hit-and-run accident; Andrea was arrested but the court withheld adjudication.

Andrea stated her strengths as a parent to be that she was "loving, honest, involved every day in [Emilie's] education, and that [she] wants to see Emilie and her dad get along." Further, her answer to the doctor's question about her weaknesses was, "I honestly don't know of any." I'm not sure how many parents could answer that way. We are human, we all make mistakes, but this was Andrea's arrogance.

She also stated that she was "happy, in good health and that she is readily accepting of the stresses that are placed upon her as a parent." Happy and accepting, two words I would never use to describe Andrea.

Andrea said that Patton's weaknesses were that he had "no routine, no set bedtime, angers easily, doesn't feed Emilie dinner all the time and that he was more concerned about how people saw him rather than being a good father." She didn't mention as his weaknesses any of the "abuse and domestic violence" problems she purported to have told the Safe Start program. Not once since I had known Patton, did he never come close to hitting or threatening to hit me or our children. I won't say he was perfect but he most definitely was a gentleman with true Christian morals who didn't believe in any physical violence. He genuinely cared about Emilie and her well-being; she was and will always be his first priority.

Dr. Boot stated in his report about Andrea that there were "no indications of significant psychopathology."

(Note: About three years after our trial, Andrea met with Dr. Boot, again. She was tested and assessed. The results were completely different the second time around. The reason she was evaluated again was another custody dispute with another father. That second time, his results were far more accurate.)

Following Andrea's assessment, Patton's results were described: Patton said that his strengths were that he makes the sacrifices that he needs to make for Emilie, he cares for her very much, he is sensitive to what she is going through, and he tries to be a good role model. He stated that his weaknesses were that he doesn't discipline her enough and lets her slide because he knows she fears her mother and also that he works a lot.

With Emilie, Dr. Boot completed several observations as well as a few other tests. On the Perception of Relationship Test (PORT), he indicated that Emilie was physiologically closer to the mother and more likely to seek her out in a time of need. On the Bricklin Perceptual Scale (BPS) Emilie was noted as perceiving both parents as being effective in handling a number of parenting situations but the mother was the parent of choice. This loyalty was a predominant characteristic of parental alienation.

Finally, on the BASC-II Self-Administered Scale as well as the Draw-A-Person test, it was indicated that Emilie was a child who "is experiencing significant depression, anxiety, and worry. She tends to internalize fears and she feels like a volcano sometimes inside." How awful for any child to feel such a thing. Patton and I had observed the same thing which was precisely why he was trying to get more time with Emilie. My stepdaughter was petrified of her mother but you would need to interview other people in Emilie's life to confirm this, which Dr. Boot chose not to do.

This was not about Patton not being a wonderful parent. This was about a little girl brainwashed and mentally abused by her mother. Emilie was being used as a pawn and at eight years old, was already "depressed." This should have indicated that Emilie being raised with her mother as the primary parent wasn't working and a change was imperative for her well-being. We were hoping the judge would see it that way.

I found Dr. Boot's conclusion to be contradictory in several places. He had stated on one page of his thirty-six page report that "It is certainly important to maintain continuity. I would most definitely recommend increased visitations with the father in the future after my recommendations are followed. Emilie is in a safe and nurturing house with the mother. There are indications that there is a great deal of conflict between Emilie and the stepmother, Lisa." There was no on-going conflict. There was one argument in the six years that I was had been a part of Emilie's life. Emilie and I adored each other but Andrea resented that and continuously attempted to alienate and alter her daughter's opinion of me.

On another page of Dr. Boot's report he said, "I see no reason or any change in circumstances to change the current custody arrangement." But, he had also recommended "increased visitation" with Patton three pages prior. I understood he commented on the alleged "conflict" that Emilie and I had but that was literally where he ended his comments regarding that.

It also wasn't fair that Dr. Boot added that he was, "unaware of any domestic violence or false information provided to the court." He, in fact, *was* aware that there were false allegations made to the police by Andrea as Patton told him. He knew these were reported to the Department of Children & Families (DCF) who report to the court for her injunction requests against Patton. All of the accusations were "unfounded" and no injunctions was ever granted for domestic violence or any other reason.

How could any doctor who didn't verify sources be allowed to give recommendations to a court of law that was presiding over the best interest of any child?

Dr. Boot's final words were analytical. "It has been concluded from many research studies that the 'single most important predictor of a child's mental health is whether or not the parents have developed effective

methods for communicating regarding their child's needs.'
Both parents must understand that the child wants to have
both of them in their life and wants to be able to love both
of them without being made to feel disloyal, secretive, or
caught in the middle. This is what is happening with
Emilie right now. This conflict will affect Emilie in a
negative way."

If only Dr. Boot knew what later happened as a result
of Andrea's ongoing emotional and physical abuse of
Emilie.

In our state, to modify custody that has already been
established, one must prove a "substantial change of
circumstances." The change to which the statute refers is
defined as being two-pronged. The first prong is that the
circumstances have changed substantially and materially
since the original custodial arrangement, and the second is
that the child's best interest justifies changing custody.
Furthermore, the substantial change must be one that was
not reasonably contemplated at the time of the original
judgment.[7] Patton never contemplated that his daughter
would be emotionally abused on a daily basis and certainly
didn't think Emilie she would be physically abused by her
mother.

Blessed is the man who remains steadfast under trial, for
when he has stood the test he will receive the crown of life,
which God has promised to those who love him.
James 1:12

XIII: Trial Time

The three-day trial began on Monday, August 3, 2009.

Patton knew it was very difficult to prove a
"substantial change of circumstances" since it was
ultimately subjective. He reminded me this was a judge,
not a jury of peers, and it could go either way. He also
reminded me that this was no longer Judge A who had
already been exposed to Andrea and her outbursts and
ruled against her on a couple of occasions during their
ongoing litigation. This was a new judge, altogether.
Judge B could be one of those "Mama Judges" and rule,
without exception, for the mother, no matter the
circumstances. Texas is one of the few, if not only, states
which allows a jury trial for certain family law issues. If
only that was the case for Patton's trial.

When Patton entered the corridor leading to the
courtroom where the trial was to be held, he saw Andrea
and a man slightly older than she sitting next to one
another. Patton recognized the man; he was the same one
who had recently gone with Andrea to a few of Emilie's
basketball and volleyball games. The man made little eye
contact this day as he had on each occasion prior. Patton
decided to go and say hello to Andrea and the gentleman
since it appeared that he was spending time with Emilie.
Emilie spoke highly of him and mentioned the fun times
the three of them had shared.

"Good morning, Andrea." Patton offered. Andrea had
no interest in replying. He somewhat expected that but
still wanted to greet the gentleman; Patton was always

polite to Andrea's boyfriends since they spent time with his daughter.

"Hello, you must be George. I have heard a lot of good things about you from my daughter; I just wanted to come over and introduce myself." Patton extended his hand for a shake and to his disappointment, George refused.

"No, I'm good," was all George said.

Patton left and went into the courtroom thinking Andrea must have painted a very dark picture of him to George since she relished in playing the victim and gaining pity.

In his opening statement, Patton, (now acting as his own attorney due to the outrageous expenses he had already incurred when he did have representation) began by telling the judge several examples of how Andrea alienated his daughter from him and interfere with his visitation. He cited the false child abuse allegations that she filed. He told how Andrea consistently disrupted the school and the administration, specifically the meeting when the principal had presented the comments (aforementioned) with the child re-enrollment consideration and how that principal herself had crossed through the word "child" and replaced it with the word "parent" then outlining the seven statements all beginning with the word "mother". Patton concluded his opening statement by saying that the parental time-sharing plan should be changed in the best interest for his "daughter's future and well-being."

Andrea was on her third attorney, Mr. Price (for whom my husband was ordered to pay). He was a short, middle-aged man with a relentless scowl on his face. Not only did he bill $20,000 to "review" the case file since he was the most recent of her legal line-up, but he continued the astronomical billing for the emails and phone calls that Andrea made as she attempted to dwindle Patton's assets. Patton and I were privy to many of those ridiculous emails and wondered how any family law attorney could stand be barraged by such nonsense. Money was the only answer.

In Mr. Price's opening, he stated how not only was my husband's opening statement more of "an argument" but that there was "anything but a substantial change in circumstances" and that "the exposure of the father of this child does more damage than good." Finally, I am sure my husband must have cringed to hear Mr. Price add to his opening "We look forward to his presentation of evidence to prove what he can prove. What we think the evidence will show is this is, with all due respect, a gentleman who ruled his marriage with an iron hand and has now attempted to rule the post-marital aspects of his daughter's life with an iron hand."

I couldn't help but recall that Andrea had not once ever suggested to the custody evaluator that my husband had any kind of "iron hand." If she or Emilie were ever truly abused, that surely would not have slipped her mind but I suppose she and her new attorney got together and that was the strategy they came up with; Patton was an abuser. Apparently this strategy was almost always the one used with parents who alienate their children.

Patton had seventeen witnesses for the three-day trial. Six of the witnesses were Emilie's teachers and from the administration office at her school. The others included her former best friend Romaine, a summer camp director, a housepainter, and others who saw firsthand Andrea's alienating behavior, and heard her tell lies about Patton and/or me.

Andrea had *no* witnesses; not even her parents came to support her. George wasn't in the actual courtroom at all. I'm sure Andrea didn't want him to see the truth about her once she saw the list of witnesses.

Some of the highlights of the trial included Emilie's teacher telling how Andrea physically removed Emilie's "cubby" from school so that the "father didn't have access to it" and, Romaine, her former best friend, telling the court several specific incidents of Andrea purposely withholding Emilie from her father as well as Andrea admitting to Romaine that she had keyed my car.

A police officer came to testify that Andrea made a false allegation about Patton abusing Emilie and that it was unfounded.

The school administrator spoke of direct statements Andrea made about Patton and his alleged abuse and his non-payment of support.

Everyone had witnessed on several occasions, Andrea's control and Emilie's discomfort. It seemed to me that the judge had no option but to rule in favor of saving this child from being raised in her dysfunctional mother's care, this was child abuse, pure and simple.

The trial was complete at 4:18 p.m. on August 5th, 2009 but there was no immediate ruling. We had to wait to receive Judge B's verdict. Three days of trial were exhausting, especially to Patton. He not only had to relive it all but anticipated the conflict and vulnerability his daughter was likely feeling each day when she got the court updates from her mother. Emilie was too young to process the duplicitous nature of her mother and the great lengths she had gone to break her bond with her daddy. Her mind already altered with delusions from her mother, Emilie, the innocent bystander in this case, was the loser no matter how the judge ruled.

Patton and I were confident that his simple request to at a minimum, change eight o'clock drop-off times twice into overnights, was not much to ask for. He wanted to be able to tuck his daughter in at night and take her to school in the morning even if it was just half of the time. All of Patton's witnesses made the case for a substantial change in circumstances if the judge considered lies, manipulations, and extreme alienation as child abuse to my stepdaughter.

"Child Abuse" as defined by 2015 Florida Statute 827.03 (b) as 1. Intentional infliction of physical or mental injury upon a child; 2. An intentional act that could reasonably be expected to result in physical or mental injury to a child; or 3. Active encouragement of any person to commit an act that results or could reasonably be expected to result in physical or mental injury to a child.[8]

Still, we wouldn't know the answer until about three weeks later.

Do your best to present yourself to God as one approved, a worker who has no need to be ashamed, rightly handling the word of truth.
    2 Timothy 2:15

XIV: The Verdict

    Judge B's Supplemental Final Judgment: No change in custody or visitation. Not enough "substantial change in circumstances" to justify a change. However, per her counterclaim, the former wife will be entitled to an additional $240 monthly in child support! This was over and above the $300 Patton had voluntarily added to his initial support.
    Where was the justice for child abuse victims? Adding fuel to the fire by tacking on additional money to be paid to a *child abuser* made no sense whatsoever.   At this point, the most recent three years of financial affidavits that Patton provided, including all tax records justified a *reduction* in support by that amount, actually more.
    Had the judge even looked at or listened to the CD Patton provided to him with the audio and visual evidence at trial? One of the days, the judge actually had his eyes closed and appeared to be taking a nap which is why Patton gave the CD to him rather than use his court time. The disk contained Andrea's threatening voicemails, video clips of Emilie speaking of her mother hitting her, and countless other recorded events, that he promised to "look at in chambers". The media proved how many times Andrea perjured herself right in front of his eyes in his courtroom under oath? She lied about so many things! What was he thinking to not help this poor child be with her father at least half of the time which also eliminated some time and exposure to her mother's calamitous manipulations, lies, alienation, and abuse? Patton told the judge in his narrative at trial that he would even continue

paying the full support amount if he did give him more time. That is how much he wanted to help his daughter live a normal life and stop Andrea's abuse.

Andrea not only won control over her daughter's life, and a permanent tool to use in her vendetta against Patton, but she would continue to build her nest egg with even more of my husband's hard earned money.

Judge B ruined my stepdaughter's life.

Patton appealed the ruling and lost again. More pain, more money, more alienation, more injustice.

If we say we have no sin, we deceive ourselves, and the truth is not in us. If we confess our sins, he is faithful and just to forgive us our sins and to cleanse us from all unrighteousness. If we say we have not sinned, we make him a liar, and his word is not in us.

1 John 1:8-10

XV: Two Men, Two Daughters, Two Trials

Andrea's dark circles and sickly face at the trial proved to be fairly normal...for a pregnant woman. Yes, Andrea had become pregnant after just one date with George, the fellow who refused Patton's handshake at the trial. During the trial, Andrea was already three months along which explained whys she was wearing disheveled untailored "bag" dresses each day. Patton, nor I, had any inkling until Emilie announced a month post-trial that she was going to have a baby sister.

George told me he met Andrea through a mutual friend who introduced them and that after a first dinner date, they went back to her house and had sex under the same premise Patton had-she was on her "cycle" and it was "okay". George found out a month later that Andrea was pregnant and Sarah was born the following February.

On the third day of the trial, Patton asked Andrea while she was on the witness stand if George was living with her.

She said, "No."

He asked if George's sixteen year old son from his previous marriage, was living with her.

She answered, "No."

Patton asked her if she received any money from George.

She answered, "No."

Although George was in the courthouse supporting his pregnant girlfriend, he was not in the court room, lest he would have heard her lie over and over again.

Less than two years later, George informed us all three of those answers were lies and that he was giving her $1100 a month while he and his teenage son resided with her during her pregnancy. We were not that surprised as it seemed nearly every word that escaped Andrea's lips was dishonest. At the time of trial or just before, Emilie had mentioned George painting a room at her mother's house so the clues were there which led to Patton's line of questioning about George during the trial in the first place.

The first time George ever spoke to Patton was by phone was when Sarah was about seven months old. He called my husband to apologize about his derogatory demeanor and his refusal to shake Patton's hand or acknowledge him at any of Emilie's games.

He told Patton that when he met Andrea she said that Patton "abused her and Emilie". He also divulged other derogatory statements that painted Andrea out to be a victim. George told Patton how Andrea said that he never paid his support on time, called his own daughter "fat," and that Emilie never liked seeing her father.

After detailing a thoughtful apology to my husband, George explained he was now going through an identical situation with his baby, Sarah. George even referred to himself as "Patton Junior."

Andrea had charmed George just like she did Patton. He unknowingly became Andrea's pawn, just as her other boyfriend's did before him. He was now living our life; one of alienation, manipulation and absence from *his* daughter's life. George would not tolerate it. He would not give up his baby daughter to that woman. One of the main reasons he left Andrea was because of the way he continuously saw how she treated Emilie. He said Andrea was controlling and always scheming. At the time, there was no other woman, no Lisa, in his story so Andrea's battle with him was strictly over control and child support, not jealousy and child support.

George and Andrea had never married each other so Andrea's alienation led George to initiate established legal custody, not modify it. When George left Andrea because he could no longer take Andrea's manipulation and lies, she decided to withhold Sarah from him altogether for several months until the hearing date came for his motion to seek custody. George was not a part of his daughter's first Halloween, Christmas, Thanksgiving, New Year or birthday.

Andrea attempted several domestic violence injunctions (restraining orders) against George but the court denied her and deemed them "unfounded" also as they had on those she filed against Patton.

Perhaps Andrea though these legal scare tactics would push his desire away from fighting for Sarah, but George, like Patton, was not backing down.

By late 2013, Andrea had filed eight false child abuse complaints against Patton and George in total.

Andrea knew that as long as DCF had an open investigation, (which typically seemed to take two to four weeks prior to a hearing date) that George was forbidden to see Sarah under a temporary injunction which was usually automatically granted the day a petitioner sought protection.

We couldn't help but blame Judge B and the Florida Family Law statutes (which were absent of acknowledging parental alienation as a form of child abuse) to be the cause of Andrea's chronic emotional abuse strategy. Judge B *allowed* this to happen by not reprimanding Andrea for her actions which essentially endorsed her grand plan to continue. The judge didn't even order Andrea to get counseling or a psychiatric evaluation. He allowed Andrea to continue to brainwash her daughter 80% of the time. Emilie at twelve was still Andrea's pawn with Patton, but was also becoming her mother's minion and ally against George. In our opinion, Judge B destroyed Emilie's life.

Sadly, this was just the beginning for George. He had no idea what he was getting himself into. His life would change until Sarah turned eighteen, not in the wonderful transformation-to-adult kind of way, but in the, you-have-no-idea-what-Andrea's-wrath-is-really-all-about way.

Turns out, we could probably have written a blueprint for George since Andrea was spreading identical lies about him that she had about Patton! Through Facebook, one of Andrea's childhood friends had confirmed this. The friend, Carla, like Romaine, said she too was finished with Andrea. Although, I was apprehensive at first about Carla maybe spying on me for Andrea, what she had written seemed sincere.

Carla and George both confirmed that Andrea's mirror-image perceptions morphed *her* actions into the actions of others.

Unfortunately, we had already seen so much injustice in Florida's family law disputes. Not only did most custody cases seem to take about two years to go to trial if they reached an impasse at mediation, but our circuit judges were often rotated among court divisions every two years.[9] This presented a huge problem for Patton since Judge A had seen Andrea for whom she really was, impulsive, out-of-control, alienating and ruthless but by the time the case got to Judge B, she learned to somewhat temper her outbursts to save face.

George was facing the same problem. The original Judge M who presided over the first year of Andrea's false accusations and hearings with him, frequently witnessed Andrea's true character and motives. He admonished her courtroom behavior just as Patton's first judge had. However, George's second Judge J was new to his case and hadn't had the benefit of seeing the real Andrea and her sophomoric, child-like conduct. This was a huge disadvantage for George, just as it had been for Patton.

But George was fortunate to catch somewhat of a break.

Dr. Boot was assigned as the custody evaluator in his case. Although it doesn't sound lucky, it was. Dr. Boot's final report this time, indicated far more accuracy about Andrea. He questioned Andrea's stability and favored George.

Some of the contradictions from Dr. Boot's second report with George and first report with Patton were:

In her second custody evaluation (CE) Andrea told Dr. Boot she had over 100 college credit hours. During Patton's CE, she told Dr. Boot that she had two years of college. At Patton's trial while she was on the stand under oath, she said she had no college courses.

Andrea admitted that she had treatment for anorexia but said it was for eight months during George's CE and for "a couple of months" during Patton's CE.

Andrea stated that the divorce with Patton was "cordial" and that they "get along well now." The reality was Andrea had been slightly "nicer" to Patton the month or two leading up to George and Andrea's trial. This was because Patton was on George's witness list and Andrea continuously asked him what he was planning to say about her. Patton simply told her, "The truth. If it benefits George or it benefits you, Andrea then I don't care, I am telling the truth in court." She still didn't provide a cell phone number for him to reach Emilie and she still didn't allow Emilie to speak with him by phone often or without the speaker, but she was slightly more flexible in trading custody time being careful not to give additional overnights that would result in more than twenty-percent. If so, it meant he could be entitled to pay less child support.

Andrea's MMPI-2 scale Psychological Test was "elevated at a very high" level in George's CE, indicating "an increased state of interpersonal sensitivity and anger. The same test during Patton's CE revealed "normal" range."

92

In George's CE, Andrea's personality profile pattern indicated someone "who is emotionally distant, rigid, opinionated, and has a hard time assuming responsibility for her problems and she tends to blame others or rationalize her faults." Spot on. Yet for some reason Dr. Boot had not drawn the same conclusion for Patton's CE.

Andrea's personality profile pattern indicated that "she is overly sensitive to criticism and can react to even minor problems with anger. She is highly suspicious of other people and her sensitivity can lead her to being argumentative. She has a tendency to hold grudges and to try to get even with those whom she thinks wronged her. She feels very insecure in relationships and to being rejected. She needs a great deal of reassurance." None of this very accurate assessment was made during Patton's CE!

The MCMI-III was administered to Andrea for George's CE and revealed that Andrea had a "high need for social approval and a definite degree of self-centered proclivity. Andrea also expects her needs to be met in an immediate manner. She is initially friendly, outgoing and even gregarious to obtain support and validation from others. When her 'emotional supplies' are frustrated, irritability and anger can ensue." How had Dr. Boot not seen this in Andrea during Patton's custody evaluation?

While meeting with Dr. Boot, Andrea told him that George was "bi-polar, has attention deficit disorder, and experiences uncontrollable anger." Although those were the same accusations she made against Patton, George provided a letter from a therapist who contradicted Andrea's accusations stating, "From my observations and discussions, I am not able to substantiate any of those accusations." The therapist further stated that there was "no clinical data to support a diagnosis of bi-polar, attention deficit disorder or irrational anger management."

Dr. Boot's final recommendation was for Andrea to "begin counseling designed to address her hypersensitivity, anger, and aggressive responding under stress. In counseling, her overly sensitive demeanor, argumentative, and resentful approach to relationships should be taken into consideration. She *alleges* having been in a number of abusive relationships with men in the past; this area should be addressed." None of this was indicated during Patton's CE and of course, Andrea didn't take the advice and seek counseling.

Dr. Boot's recommendation for George was to "participate in counseling to improve his ability to communicate more effectively with Andrea and better understand his role in the family conflict. He also can develop better coping mechanisms in dealing with stressful situations."

Dr. Boot concluded his report by recommending that a court-appointed parent coordinator (PC) be available until the parents are better able to communicate and cooperate effectively. He also suggested the PC be permitted to testify if they went to trial.

People often suggest that we ask Dr. Boot to prepare an amendment to Patton's CE. That would be nice but we would have to start the battle all over, spending tens of thousands of dollars that we no longer have.

George and Andrea, like Patton and Andrea, began to use the services of a parent coordinator (PC). Patton and Andrea's PC, Dr. K, had been no help in their case, just another $10,000 bill that Patton had to pay for zero resolution and Andrea's non-compliance to his directives. George and Andrea's PC was a little bit better.

Their PC quickly noticed Andrea's resentment, manipulations and control over little Sarah. George told me that Andrea would banter back and forth with the PC sometimes their entire hour session. The PC would continually tell Andrea, "You just don't get it." She also classified Andrea's actions as "alienating" while proposing she get counseling. Per usual, Andrea did not.

The PC ultimately ruled that George's visitation with Sarah every other Saturday night plus a few hours on Wednesday that Andrea was allowing should change to

94

overnights Friday through Monday every other weekend while his Wednesdays were turned into overnights, as well.

Andrea was livid!

"That's not what I have with my ex-husband!" Andrea complained. The PC told her, "Well, he should."

While George's case was in litigation, Andrea's angst was taking its toll on Emilie. Andrea had developed a partner in Emilie who could assist in bashing George and the wonderful relationship he had with Sarah. Emilie began to sound like her mother, describing how awful George was. Sarah was just three years old so she didn't speak much for herself but her words to the DCF during the many false abuse allegations investigations reeked of coaching by Andrea. That coaching, was evident each time, which is probably why each of the injunction petitions against George were closed, "unfounded". The case manager on those allegations later testified on George's behalf at one of their hearings.

Emilie shared with Patton and me that that George hit Sarah and was "mean to her mom." Not wanting Emilie involved, Patton was always diplomatic in his responses to Emilie and asked if she ever witnessed that herself to which she replied, "No, but my mom tells me."

Patton suggested that Emilie judge George as he was, not as anyone told her he was. He reminded Emilie of all the wonderful times she had with him fishing and playing basketball and just hanging out. He reminded her of how she used to say when she was mad at Patton that she "wished George was her dad!" Patton was fair-minded and encouraged his daughter to base her opinion of a person on what she felt, not on what someone else felt or what they (Andrea) told her to feel/think. He wanted her to stay out of George's and Andrea's problems and litigation and instead focus on her own life and being a kid.

Our bond with George, Sarah, and his children from his first family began to strengthen. Once again, like

Romaine, our new friendship with George emerged from conflict with Andrea. In fact, Patton and I included George, Sarah, and George's son, over for Sarah's second birthday so Emilie could see how our families managed to get along well sans Andrea. It was awkward at first for Emilie because she was then so programmed to loathe George, but after adjusting and accepting him, she did great and really enjoyed the get-together.

That was almost two years ago. I can safely say that our relationship with Emilie had been steadily improving once Andrea's sights were now set on destroying George and his bond with their daughter, Sarah. Regardless of the reason, I was happy that Emilie was beginning to be less negative at our home. The less acrimony there was, the happier and more stable she appeared to feel. Andrea's focus was still alienating and negative toward Patton but her energy was mostly exerted in her battle with George. That was another $1200 in child support she was receiving. With Patton's increased support and George's support, Andrea made the equivalent of a professional earning $50k a year! These children were nothing but a meal ticket to her.

Patton was keeping Emilie busy with golf lessons, practices, and tournaments. Emilie and I also grew closer as Emilie matured and began to think for herself a bit more. Her mother was so focused on indoctrinating Emilie to have hatred toward George, she all but forgot to continue alienating her from me—until Emilie told her mother about George coming to our house with Sarah for her birthday.

We were completely back to square one.

Emilie was a part of a recreational basketball league but abruptly began telling us that she didn't want me to go watch her play anymore because it stressed out her mother. She did the same with her track meets. After plenty of calls from Andrea to Patton about the games and my presence, I decided not to go. I was hurt and equally angry. Tension in my marriage resurfaced. The alienation polluted Emilie's mind and something as simple as deciding a restaurant for dinner or picking out a movie turned into a ridiculous argument. Patton would always feel bad if Emilie had a negative attitude. While on occasion he did admonish her negative words and tone, ultimately, he would find a way to blame it on everything she had been through with her mother's emotional abuse. I didn't necessarily disagree but I did privately point out to him that she was a preteen and did know the difference between right and wrong. His constant justification of her behavior felt a bit like déjà vu; he was now, to some degree, enabling her. This is exactly what I felt he did with Andrea for so long and now Emilie? Our family was once again in chaos.

Patton committed to helping make Emilie's life as enjoyable and stress-free as he could at our home. He immersed himself in Emilie's physical and athletic interests to help boost her self-esteem and preoccupy her. He taught her how to play golf and she loved it. Unfortunately our family dinners together became rare as Emilie suddenly seemed to only desire spend time with Patton, not McKenna or me.

Emilie was doing terrific in golf, actually. She was a natural as she had been with nearly every sport! Several junior tournaments, numerous costly private lessons, and months later, Emilie sharply announced that she was no longer interested in golf. Her mother hadn't liked that that was all she did with Patton. Per Emilie, Andrea told her, "it [wasn't] healthy" and sadly, Emilie still being brainwashed, agreed. Patton was as infuriated as he was puzzled. Why would Andrea discourage golf? She had been totally supportive initially (possibly because she realized I wasn't joining them on the links). Nothing made sense about this except that it had to be alienation.

Soon, more of Andrea's manipulations surfaced. Emilie began to threaten Patton. "If you testify for George, dad, I won't come over and visit anymore!" Patton reminded her that she shouldn't be put in the middle and told Andrea to stop doing this to Emilie. Phone conflicts quickly became fairly regular.

Emilie's love toward me changed once again in just a matter of days. It broke my heart. I had teared up with pride watching my stepdaughter trying so hard at her track meets and now, she "hated me" for no reason. I loaned her a pretty blouse, my pearl necklace from my grandmother, and styled her hair for a birthday party she attended a couple of days earlier. But Andrea's influence and Emilie's loyalty to her mother reemerged as her priority.

"Dad, can you tell Lisa and McKenna not to come to my meet next week?" She would ask her father.

"Emilie, you loved having Lisa there, you were right next to her most of the time. Why do you suddenly not want her to come?" Patton inquired thoughtfully.

"Well, Lisa is just mean and I don't even like her." Emilie said.

"What are you talking about? You two were playing basketball together a few hours ago and making meatballs before that. Plus, she helped you get all ready for your party. What are you talking about, Emilie?"

"Well, it is just that my mom wants to go but my mom *won't* go if Lisa is there, and I want my mom to go." Emilie relayed.

"So your mom and Lisa can both go, who cares?"

"But my mom said she will be all stressed and doesn't want to go if she is there." Emilie admitted.

"Emilie that is something your mom needs to worry about, not you. Why would she or you care if Lisa came to support you? There are hundreds of people at those meets...if your mom doesn't want to say hello to Lisa then fine but you should not tell Lisa she shouldn't go." Patton reasoned.

"But if Lisa is going then I am not going to go—I won't go on the bus to the meet and won't be there." Emilie threatened.

Patton later confronted Andrea about this but she denied having any influence, saying that Emilie didn't like me.

The alienation was kicking back in full force for Patton, too. Around homework time one night, Patton and Emilie argued about her blatant disobedience. That is when she threatened Patton not to visit anymore if he "testified for George."

Emilie had the principal of her school call Patton the following Monday to say she didn't want to see him and not to pick her up. Emilie had never done that! Her mother put her up to that, we later found out. But Patton didn't exercise his visitation that day as he knew the stress it would cause for his daughter.

Patton and I were on thin ice with Emilie but a few days after that, I was ready to speak my mind. I thought about my words being twisted so I decided to turn on the audio recorder in my phone.

I told Emilie how proud I was of her and how much I loved that our relationship had gotten so much better the past year or two. I then asked her why she would ever not want me to attend any of her events or functions and reminded her that I had been a part of her life for more than ten years. I told her how I felt that she was being put up to this malice toward me and asked her why? She answered, "Well because you are friends with George." It seemed the birthday celebration of Sarah's at our house and her mother's disapproval of blending our families was to what her new attitude was attributed.

"Emilie I am not 'friends with George,' I am more of an acquaintance. There is nothing wrong with that, in fact I wish that you and your mom were friendly with him for all of your sakes, and especially Sarah's! You do realize that if something, God forbid, ever happened to your mother that Sarah would go to live with him permanently, right? Well, I am glad to be friendly with him to keep the line of communication open so that if something did happen, you would have a way to spend time with your

99

little sister. You should never be put in the middle and I hate that you are. Doesn't that bother you? I mean, how does that make you feel?" I finally exhaled.

"I know but I *am* in the middle, I can't help it." Emilie quietly answered looking down as if she were embarrassed or hurt or both.

"Right, but you shouldn't be! Have you thought of standing up for yourself and telling your mom to stop putting you there?" I asked compassionately.

"Yes, like two weeks ago I asked her to stop putting me in the middle." Emilie confided.

"And what did she say?" I asked ever so softly so she knew I was asking out of concern and pity, not spite or anger.

"She just said, 'Well too bad, you are there and you're going to listen.'" I was surprised Emilie told me this. I wished she would always open up to me. I was always there for her, but she wasn't allowed to be disloyal to her mother.

I offered my sympathy but I implored her not to throw me or her dad under the bus. I gave Emilie, who looked to be a little humbled, a hug. I reminded her I loved her, and I was proud of her. She responded kindly and the night got better. What a shame to see a twelve-year-old be so frightened of her own mother! At her height of five-foot-seven and her amazing strength, I was actually surprised. Why was she so fearful of her mother's punishment, how bad could it be?

Our annual trip to Aspen in late March, 2013 gave some clarity to Emilie's fluctuating temperament. Emilie had a black eye when my husband picked her up for vacation. In the car, following the pick-up, Patton inquired how she had received it. Emilie told him that it was when she was tickling her sister.

When I saw the eye, I was immediately suspicious but wanted to mask my concern. I inquired more matter of factly, "Oh my goodness, what happened to you silly?"

Emilie's story was different, "I was wrestling with my sister, and she accidentally kicked me." I accepted that as truthful but was still a bit suspicious. A few minutes later, when Patton and I were able to have a private conversation in our cramped, but private, walk-in closet, I asked my husband if he believed the wrestling with Sarah story in regards to the black eye. He quickly jerked his head to me and asked me if I was sure that is what she told me. I confirmed it, and he told me the tickling story she had just shared with him in the car. We were both convinced that something wasn't right. You don't change your story when it was truthful, we agreed, but we also had just twenty minutes or so before leaving for the airport to catch our flight. Patton didn't call the police or DCF; he wanted to be sure that we weren't wrong before filing any abuse allegations.

Once in Aspen, we made sure to get photos of Emilie to document the black eye. My father, his girlfriend and a visiting friend all noticed the eye right away, but Emilie just minimized it, "Yeah, my little sister and I were playing."

A few days into the trip, per usual, Emilie's closeness toward us grew, and her guard dropped. She always got closer to Patton and me once she was away from her mother's influence. Patton took advantage of her tenderness and after asking if her eye was still hurting, he asked exactly how it happened.

"My sister and I were playing airplane and her foot kicked me accidentally in the eye but I don't want to talk about it anymore." Two red flags in one sentence: another variation of the story and not wanting to talk about it anymore.

Patton wanted answers. "Wait a minute." Patton said. "So, show me. If you are holding Sarah up like this (he demonstrated) and her feet are back there, how did her foot reach all the way forward to your eye when you are five-foot-seven. It doesn't make sense."

"Dad, I already told you what happened, and I don't want to talk about it anymore. Sarah did it." Emilie said finitely.

Two and a half months later, everything changed.

Emilie in Aspen with faded blackeye.

But if anyone does not provide for his relatives, and especially for members of his household, he has denied the faith and is worse than an unbeliever.

1 Timothy 5:8

XVI: Arrest in Development

Emilie's last day of school, Friday, June 5th, 2013, was a half day. Emilie had one of her last final exams in seventh grade that day. To most kids, the last day of school was a joyous one, even memorable! It was only the latter for my stepdaughter.

This was also Patton's weekend so he was to pick her up directly after school which was in session only until noon. However, on this morning, Andrea actually called Patton to tell him how horrible Emilie's attitude had been and how she had been talking back to her, even suggesting her menstrual cycle was the reason for Emilie's foul demeanor. She asked Patton to not get her from school but instead to pick her up at three o'clock from the bank drop-off location they used when school wasn't in session. He reluctantly agreed.

When it came time for Patton to pick Emilie up, Andrea stalled and said she was running late in bringing Emilie to drop off. Patton never bothered to ask why anymore for Andrea would either ignore it, hang up, or say she had another call coming in, if not some other excuse. It was close to 5:30 that evening before Andrea finally brought Emilie to the bank. As soon as Emilie was in the car, my husband noticed scratch marks on her face and asked where they came from.

"I don't have any scratches," Emilie defiantly responded.

"Yes, you do, look in the mirror." Patton pulled down the sun visor so she could see in the mirror.

When Emilie got home she walked right up to me and asked, "Hey Lisa, do you see any scratches on my neck?" She was almost asking me to notice them.

I put my glasses on to get a better look. "Yes, I see a scratch on your neck, and faint ones on your cheek. Where are they from?"

"My sister and I were playing..." Emilie droned.

My husband felt in his heart that the truth was yet to come so he pressed on. "Honey, I want to know where you got those." Patton asked more vigilantly.

"Sarah kicked me. That's it!" Emilie roared back.

"Honey, I am not trying to upset you, I am only trying to get you to tell me what is going on. Those scratches are not from a foot; they are from fingernails. You always seem to blame Sarah for any bruise, black-eye or marks you have, I just want to protect you from anyone who might be hurting you." Patton spoke softly but with conviction.

Knowing that George also had his weekend with his daughter, Sarah, I called him privately to inquire if Sarah mentioned anything. George mentioned that Andrea was an hour late for the drop-off of his daughter, too.

Sarah was actually in the car with him at the time of my call so George nonchalantly asked, "Sarah, what happened to Emy's face, honey. Did you and your sister play or fight today?"

"Mommy hit Emy, Daddy!" I heard her say.

George asked how and what she did.

"Emy said stop hitting me, Mommy!" Sarah explained, making a cat-like motion with her hands as if playing with a ball of yarn.

When I told Patton what I had just heard from George and Sarah, he was devastated. It confirmed his worst fear that Andrea was also physically abusive to his daughter. He was angry of course at Andrea, but so sad for Emilie who suffered, and Sarah who had seen it all.

The rest of the weekend my husband couldn't sleep well, and my stepdaughter was having nightmares. Patton

104

needed Emilie to agree to be honest with the police or DCF. Thankfully, Andrea told Patton he could actually keep Emilie Sunday night even though that was typically when Emilie went back to her mother's house every other weekend. Andrea had been unusually generous to Patton this week, which happened to precede the upcoming custody trial she had with George. She even asked the week before if he would like to keep Emilie for overnights throughout the trial week since it was on the docket from Tuesday through Thursday. Patton would be called as a witness on Thursday morning at her trial with George.

Patton loved the extra time! And he was determined to build Emilie's faith that he would do whatever he could to protect her from any more bruises, black-eyes and abrasions from her mother. Emilie was going to have to agree to testify against her mom. After a decade of lies and manipulations by Andrea, it wouldn't be easy.

During her extended visitation, Patton probed Emilie again. With heartfelt concern, he asked Emilie to admit the truth about the scratches. Emilie looked at his phone to be sure he wasn't recording her. "Honey, I am not recording you. I just want to help you. If your mom is doing this to you, it is wrong and I don't ever want her to do it again. But you have to tell me so that I can help you. I am already convinced that your mom is abusing you, but what I don't know is the frequency with which it is occurring." Patton pleaded.

"How do you know?" Emilie asked.

"I just do." Patton said simply.

"But dad, if I tell you how often it happens, then I am admitting that my mom does it." Emilie was a thinker.

"Honey, I just want you to live a happy and healthy life. I want to you to be a kid and enjoy your childhood. Child abuse is serious and should never happen and I am going to make sure it never happens to you again!" Patton implored.

"But what can you do dad? She said that if I ever told you that I would never get to see you again! I would rather just take it and be able to see you." Emilie's love for my husband was greater than any of us conceived.

"I will make sure she never does it again; don't worry about that. I just need you to be honest. Was the black-eye just before the Aspen trip really from your sister?"

"No."

"Emilie, I need to know how these came about. What made your mom feel the need to hit you? I mean was there a reason?" Patton inquired.

Referring to the last day of school Emilie explained. "Well, Friday, she wanted me to go for a run on before school. She always makes me run. As soon as I woke up, she told me to get my clothes on for school and then when I went to wash my face, she told me to run instead. I was mad and told her I wanted to wash my face and didn't want to run since I had to go to school and was already wearing my school shirt and jeans."

Emilie left no detail out. "She told me to 'watch my attitude and get out there and run, not walk!' After my run, she was standing in front of the house waving the phone at me and she was talking all nice to you. I asked her why she was being all fake to you. Then, I said hi to you and after the phone call I went into the house and she told me what a bad attitude I had. She told Sarah to wait on the couch in the living room and told me to go in her room. She pushed me down on her bed and began slapping me while I was trying to explain that I didn't do anything wrong. After she saw she had scratched my face and you could see it, she was going to keep me home from school but I told her I had to go, that it was that last day of school and that I had my last final exam!"

"Did Sarah see anything?"

"Yeah, she left the door open and Sarah peeked in and my mom yelled at her to go back to the couch. I was being a smart mouth so I probably deserved it." Emilie shrugged.

"No! Nobody deserves to be treated like that. That is exactly what child abuse victims feel, like they 'deserve' it. You didn't deserve to be hit or punched; you never do. No child does!" Patton fired back.

Patton fought the tears welling up in his eyes. He shared something that he never thought he would.
"Honey, I know what it is like to live with your mother..."

"I know Dad, but you got to leave and get a divorce, I have to stay there and I hate it. It is like the rules don't apply to her, like she does whatever she wants and gets away with it!" Emilie interrupted.

Patton led Emilie into the house to our bedroom and opened the top drawer of his armoire where he pulled out an old yellow and black envelope. He opened it and pulled out about a dozen photographs. He showed them to Emilie. They were the photos of Patton's tattered clothes, bloody face, and fat lip after one of Andrea's altercations with him. I say "her" altercation because my husband didn't dare fight back and risk losing his license to practice law, over Andrea. He explained that the photos were taken at the beginning of their second month of marriage.

Patton went on to explain that although the police were involved, he never formally pressed charges against Andrea. He was "too soft," was the only reason he gave.

After Patton showed the photos to Emilie, I privately made some suggestions to him as to what I would do. I encouraged him to record Emilie (so she didn't later deny her confessions because she feared her mother's wrath) and then do what Andrea had always done.

Every time, Andrea (falsely) accused George or Patton of child abuse, temporary injunctions were implemented the same day. Neither was permitted to have any visitation with their respective daughters until the hearing date where the judge would make a determination to grant or dismiss the motion.

As we learned, Andrea's feeble attempts to alienate the fathers of her children (by lying, in her case) were still a brief victory for Andrea; she was able to have two to three straight weeks of uninterrupted brainwashing time with her daughters until the hearing took place.

Patton vacillated back and forth with his options. By Monday, he decided to contact one of the detectives who were involved in investigating Andrea for making false abuse allegations against George. Once he spoke with the detective, they agreed that calling the Abuse Hotline and filing the restraining order would be best to do under the circumstances. Patton was worried that Emilie wouldn't speak to the authorities but he was wrong. Emilie was ready to talk; she *finally* wanted her mother stopped.

During the next few days we heard "Dad, are you sure I won't have to go back to my mom's house?" and "You promise?" and even "I never want to go back…ever!" One time I tried to temper her anger and pain.

"Honey, you know, if she got counseling, got the help she needed, she might turn out to be much nicer to you and you will regret saying you never want to see her again, you know?" I suggested calmly even though I didn't believe my own words.

"No, I honestly don't care if I ever saw her again she would only be nice for like an hour or day or something. She is so fake!" Emilie retorted.

Assured that she would not go home to her mother's house and her mom could not control or abuse her anymore, Emilie became a much happier person, more relaxed and less complex. Once she opened her mother's box of secrets, she seemed to find sharing from it cathartic as the burden of hiding and lying about so much over the past years dissipated. Random memories of lying, uncontrolled temper and acts of violence spewed from Emilie's lips over the next few days. At first, Emilie asked her father to not share with me everything she told him but then I guess she wanted me to know, and then McKenna, too!

Emilie, I believe finally began to be herself, trust in our family, and have faith in our protection and conviction against her mother's abuse. We learned quite a lot about what Emilie was made to do over the past few years and her penalties for refusing to be obedient or forgetting to do what was asked of her by her mother.

Among several dozen recollections, Emilie admitted that her mother pulled at her arm and hand making her wrist "pop" on several occasions. Patton had been taking her to see specialists for nearly a year because of the enigmatic pain in her wrist! She even wore a cast for some time while the doctors tried to determine what specifically her injury was.

She shared with us how her mom often sent her and her little sister out in the back yard. She locked them out of the house refusing to let them come in for water even after a couple of hours sometimes. Emilie would knock on the door wanting a drink and her mother would shrug her away. She said all her mom would do was talk on the phone or go on the computer.

Emilie shared several recent stories of her mother making dramatic scenes at Supercuts, Krispy Kreme and other local venues. She would yell, argue, and curse at employees and management. She drove erratically, running traffic lights and stop signs. Physically, the punishment was all on Emilie, not Sarah. Andrea would grab her, throw her against the wall, pinch and grab her arms leaving bruises, slap her in the face, and pinch her tongue.

Emilie told us how one summer she had attended the free middle school camp at a local recreational center. When she went in upset and with a black eye, one of the administrators tried to get her to open up about where it came from, but she didn't tell him. Emilie confirmed the emotional and mental challenges her mother asked of her: keep quiet and don't tell anyone anything that happens at home and use Sarah as an excuse if ever marks are noticed. Sarah bore witness to several incidents but was too little to speak up about it, or perhaps like Emilie she too, was threatened with not seeing *her* dad if she told anyone.

All this time Emilie appeared to have such an off-putting and negative attitude at our house, but it was really just a place where she could finally release some semblance of emotion, how she was truly feeling without emotional consequences or physical repercussions. It all made sense now. Obviously, Emilie did want to spend her time with Patton since not being able to see him appeared to be the punishment if Emilie told anyone of her lies or abuse. All of these admissions just had to help my stepdaughter free herself from the last decade of emotional and physical abuse. Any judge, going forward could no longer turn a blind eye.

Tuesday, Patton picked up the lengthy paperwork from the courthouse to file a motion for an injunction for Emilie against her mother.

On Wednesday morning, Patton had a hearing for one of his clients in Leesburg, Florida, about two hours away. On his drive back, he called the Abuse Hotline and filed his report on Andrea. He arrived back in town and promptly went to the courthouse at just about 3:55pm only to find that they weren't accepting any more filings that day; he would have to file the next morning instead. The next morning was also the day he was expected at the same courthouse for George and Andrea's custody trial.

No one could have prepared any of us for what happened the next day.

There are six things that the Lord hates, seven that are an abomination to him: haughty eyes, a lying tongue, and hands that shed innocent blood, a heart that devises wicked plans, feet that make haste to run to evil, a false witness who breathes out lies, and one who sows discord among brothers.

Proverbs 6:16-19

XVII: Thursday the Thirteenth

On Thursday, June 13, 2013, Patton was in the courthouse by 9:30 a.m. to file an emergency motion for temporary custody/supervised visitation, the appointment of a Guardian Ad Litem for Emilie, and an injunction against Andrea on Emilie's behalf. Following that, he walked down the hall to enter the judge's chambers for George and Andrea's custody trial. Patton was asked only one question by Andrea's attorney. He was asked if it was true that he and Andrea disagreed over the frequency that Emilie should play golf. That was it. I don't know what that had to do with Sarah and her best interest?

George's attorney was brief also and asked only a few questions of my husband being careful to keep the scope on the custody issue of George and Andrea. Basically his goal was to unveil their co-parenting ability. Patton said his co-parenting with Andrea had been good for the past few months, but he noted it had not been good prior.

Almost at the same time Patton walked into the courthouse to file his motion, the doorbell at our house rang. It was Child Protective Services (CPS). There was one investigator and one sheriff, a woman and man, respectively.

I led them to the living room where they interviewed Emilie. She wasn't nervous; she was very succinct and forthright. After a few minutes of over-hearing her speak with conviction and strength, I decided to give them full

111

privacy and left to walk our dog. I was gone for close to fifteen minutes. When I came back in, they were just wrapping up. I was next.

I probably reiterated the information that Emilie already gave but answered all the questions regarding abuse and marks on her body to the best of my recollection. I also mentioned the emotional aspect of Andrea's alienation and explained that custody had been an issue from the first day I met my husband more than a decade ago. I explained how she had falsely accused both fathers of child abuse numerous times as what I believed to be a parental alienation tactic. Emotional abuse had always been apparent and I added that Emilie, and probably her little sister, Sarah, would have a lifetime of issues because of it.

The investigator was candid. The fact that the black eyes, scratches, and bruises were no longer visible made them hard to use against Andrea. The investigator referenced a case whereby a boy was hurt with an electrical cord by his mother. CPS got him into a safe place for just one day but the next day, after the mother admitted that she just "snapped," the boy was back at home with his mom.

How could this be? This made no sense at all! Did it take a bullet hole or hatchet blow to protect innocent, abused children? I felt sick and disheartened but didn't want to react as I knew I had to stay strong and confident for Emilie.

Surely the judge would at least grant a temporary injunction given all the information Patton had written in the detailed report he filed that morning. We had to bank on that since emergency motions for injunctions were either granted temporarily or denied in the same business day.

When Patton left the courtroom, he stopped by the judge's office briefly and then came home. Riddled with questions from Emilie, he answered each one composedly.

"Did you file the restraining order, Dad?" She asked first. "What did they ask you in George's trial? Did you tell them what she has been doing to me? Was she there? Am I going to have to see her today? She said she wants me back today after the trial, after she calls! I don't want to go back, Dad!" Emilie was terrified and a nervous wreck. Fear was the only emotion Emilie seemed to have left in her.

Patton reassured her that there was no way that he was giving her back to her mother until her mother got the help she needed and that would take some time, if treatment or counseling would even work.

Emilie generally got moodier by the hour just before she had to see her mother. But this day was different; she was more worried than I had *ever* seen her. She kept reiterating over and over that she did not want to go back to her mother, ever. It was hard to console her without knowing if CPS had talked to Andrea and banned her from contact with her children, and we had no indication either way.

The ruling on the injunction came early that evening.
Denied.

This was unbelievable! Here was a child who had to keep her mouth shut for almost a decade and now she was ready and willing to testify against her mother's brutality. How could any judge (let alone, two or three judges) continue to allow such emotional and (now confirmed by an intelligent young adult) physical child abuse for so many years? Andrea *fabricated* abuse allegations against George and Patton yet her injunctions were *always* temporarily granted the same day on which they she filed them.

My husband, an attorney, and me, a mom, lost faith in Florida family law. It looked as though Andrea would *never* suffer a consequence for any of her repulsive behaviors thanks to the permission of our legal system.

Once Patton broke the bad news to Emilie, she was devastated; she thought it would have been at least a

113

couple of weeks before she would have to see her mother, if she ever did. Patton contacted his attorney Scott, whom he hired for the motions he filed that day, to ask if he was legally permitted to keep his daughter at our home even though the Marital Settlement Statement said that Thursdays were the mother's custodial time. Given that he had filed the report with the Abuse Hotline and with the courts, Scott reassured Patton that he was well within his right to protect his child.

Florida Statute 787.03 is what I have copied below directly from their website:

(4a) It is a defense that "The defendant had reasonable cause to believe that his or her action was necessary to preserve the minor or incompetent person from danger to his or her welfare.

Further, that statute reads:

(4b) The defendant was the victim of an act of domestic violence or had reasonable cause to believe that he or she was about to become the victim of an act of domestic violence as defined in s. 741.28, and the defendant had reasonable cause to believe that the action was necessary in order for the defendant to escape from, or protect himself or herself from, the domestic violence or to preserve the minor or incompetent person from exposure to the domestic violence.[10]

About six-thirty or so that evening, Andrea called and Patton picked up the phone after her third attempt. He was vague and neutral-toned when he told her he wasn't giving Emilie back to her that evening. I could hear Andrea screaming repeatedly with the same few questions that Patton was not ready to answer. Apparently, CPS never made it over to Andrea's that day so she was oblivious to any of the information he had reported to the authorities.

"What do you mean you aren't bringing her to me? Patton, what kind of game are you playing? What's going on?" She repeated.

"Andrea, I am not going to get into this right now, you will know tomorrow, but for now, I will tell you that Emilie is safe, and she will be staying here with me." He told her calmly. I don't know how he stayed so calm, but he was always in control of his temperament. That wasn't good enough for Andrea.

"I want to talk to Emilie, get her on the phone!" She insisted.

"Emilie is outside right now, I will tell her that you want to speak to her and if she wants to call you, she is always welcome to." Patton reasoned before closing out the call.

Patton went out back where Emilie was sitting on the top of the seawall and appeared to be in deep thought. He approached her to let her know that he had spoken with Andrea and exactly what was said. Emilie said she wasn't going to call her mother; she had nothing to say to her.

The next hour or so, Emilie's posture loosened up and her conversation voice became softer and less stressed sounding. She appeared to have found a little peace knowing that even though she was furious about the judge denying the injunction and disappointed that CPS didn't seem to have much hope in keeping her from her mother, her dad still professed his dedication and commitment to keeping her there at our house until she felt safe and could trust her mother whether that meant weeks, months, or years.

I suggested to Emilie that she start an Instagram® account to get her mind off of those things. Her mother previously made her delete her social accounts when McKenna asked to "friend" her. I reminded her that while she was in our care, and as long as Daddy was okay with Instagram®, that she could have an account. She, at first worried about her mother finding out and then after Patton verbally approved and assured her that it was okay, decided to set one up. That occupied her for a bit as did McKenna, who helped her take some photos for an hour or so. In fact, the girls had been taking "selfies" together by the window in McKenna's room with what little remaining sunset light there was when McKenna abruptly announced that Andrea was walking outside of our house!

Emilie practically flew to our master bedroom on the other side of the house to hide. We closed all of the plantation shutters and turned the lights off but the entire back of our home faced Tampa Bay and we didn't use blinds or any window dressings that would cover the view. Andrea pressed her face against the glass as she looked in. She attempted to open the sliding glass door but thankfully it was locked. She continued to walk around the perimeter and to the front courtyard. She banged on the front door and attempted to lift the handle which was also locked. Emilie was an emotional disaster hovered in the corner of our room. It was terrifying to see a child so fearful; we actually were all uncomfortable and a little nervous. Patton reassured us that there was no way she was coming into our house and taking her. He would not let that happen. Emilie still trembled in terror.

While we were calming my stepdaughter, Andrea walked around to the back sliding door and again tried to open it.

Andrea appeared to give up and we watched from a crack in between the shutters as she entered her car and finally drove away.

A half-hour or so later, I suggested that my husband go move his car that he had temporarily parked on the street. Bicycles and my car took up the garage but from experience, I feared that Andrea might try to vandalize or key Patton's vehicle on the open road. He agreed and went out to move it into the driveway.

When Patton got into the car to move it, Andrea ran on foot out of nowhere and raced to get into our home. She almost succeeded in getting into the house. Luckily Patton got there at the same time. She only managed to get half of her body over the threshold while Patton safely guarded her from getting all the way in.

She called out in her phony charm voice. "Emilie, come here, honey. Diane wants to talk to you." Hearing that, Patton noticed a small white SUV (not her green BMW) in front of our house now.

Diane was Andrea's next door neighbor whom Emilie assured was always nice to her. It didn't matter, Emilie wanted nothing to do with her mother and she was adamant about not leaving the safety of our bedroom.

As Patton verbally worked Andrea out of our front doorjamb, I overheard her say that the police were on their way. Patton replied that he was glad; he had plenty to tell them.

A few minutes later, three police officers came to the door. There was one female donning a basic pony tail but looking very serious who looked to be about thirty-something years old, a burly, middle-aged wrestler looking man and a slim fellow who appeared young enough to possibly be a rookie. Patton stayed in the house while he spoke with them through our opened front door. They weren't allowed to enter the house without a search warrant so there was no way they were coming in to our home for any reason especially to take his daughter away and place her in the care of the person he had already reported was abusing her.

As I approached the bedroom to check on Emilie and McKenna, I hit the record button on my phone to document Emilie's words so that later, when Andrea twisted the events of the night, as I knew she did with everything and anything, I would have a copy of the facts.

"Dad's talking to the police; I am just letting you know." I told Emilie calmly.

"Gosh!" Emilie said angrily.

"Well, they probably want to check on you honey, okay?" I assured her.

"Yeah, dad said they …talk to me right now so….say that you" I can't recall what her exact words were and the sound wasn't clear on the audio, but she was asserting that she shouldn't have to speak to them anymore since she had talked to them early that morning at the CPS interview.

"Did my-is my mom out there?" She asked.

"Yeah, she's out there. He told me to record it but they're outside so-don't worry about it." I said.

"I'll go outside!" McKenna offered vehemently. Although they weren't super close in a friendship kind of way, they were still family and McKenna hated seeing Emilie so distressed.

"No, stay put." I told my daughter.

"I'm not talking to them in front of my mom, that's not happening, I'm sorry. I'm not coming out of this house. I'm not coming out when she's right there. No, that's not happening. No." The recording captured the fear in Emilie's words.

"That's okay, you don't have to." I agreed.

"I'm not talking to them." Emilie repeated.

"I understand." I told her.

"You should talk to them." McKenna suggested.

"You need to let them know..." I started before McKenna interrupted.

"You need to say it right in front of her face so she knows what she's doing." McKenna told Emilie.

"Or you let them know that you'll talk to them if your mom is away. If that's how you feel, then you need to tell them what you feel, honey. And, tell them why you feel that way." I offered.

"I'm not doing it in front of my mom." Emilie said again.

"Then just ask her to leave. Tell Dad to tell her to leave," McKenna said as she ate her cereal (her dinner that night since while we were in hiding from Andrea, we had access to only the food pantry of our house).

The three of us, still hovered in the corner of my master bedroom on the floor, tried to calm each other. Emilie's mind was going a mile a minute as she was speaking so rapidly. "I already talked to someone today and I thought that would be all I had to do, so that's stupid." Emilie said.

"It's going to be alright honey. It's going to be alright." I said as I left the room to check on the conversation Patton was having with the police at the door.

With Andrea nowhere in sight, Emilie finally came to the door and I pushed my record button again while standing behind the door. The recording went as follows:

"Okay, here she is, you can talk to her." Patton said as his arm barricaded Emilie's body from the police, preventing them from reaching in to take her.

"Can you come and talk to us?" The officer asked.

"You can talk to her right there; I'm not going to say anything." Patton assured them.

"I'll let you talk to her." The officer responded.

"She'll talk to you right now; she's going to be afraid..." Patton said firmly.

"I'm not afraid. I've told him everything that I'm going to tell you. I'm just scared to tell everything to my mom." Emilie said calmly.

"You don't want to be with your mom?" The policeman asked.

"I do NOT want to see her again." Emilie emphatically declared.

"And why is that?" He continued.

"She scares me, I mean she's gotten physical with me, she's given me a black eye, she scratches me in the face, and she scratched me on the neck..." Emilie spoke nervously but with conviction.

"Now listen, listen, I'm not here to try to give someone... to you know make someone go where they don't want to be. You know, I don't want to see someone get hurt." The officer assured her.

"I know but you said we've gotta go by the paperwork, and I said, 'if you are here to enforce a civil...you can't come in our house...'" Patton interjected.

"I can't come in your house and grab her." The officer responded.

"Well, I wouldn't think so," Patton agreed.

"I'm not stupid; I don't want to lose my job."

"I don't know what is left to do." Patton said.

"She may be able to go file a civil..."

"She can go do whatever she wants to do; I'm gonna be a dad to her and protect her." Patton conveyed.

"I respect what you say. You're trying to be a dad and protect her, that's great. I'm actually helping to raise some teenage girls myself and I know what it is like, I know what you're going through." Patton didn't respond to this so the officer went on. "Like I said we're not gonna come inside your house and take her so answer your door from now on, okay?" But he still wasn't leaving.

"You're not gonna say anything about like me not wanting to see her because if I… if she finds out about that she'll probably like go…" Emilie paused, "um hitting on me."

"If she tries to come in here and grab you, she's going to be breaking the law."

"Well she's already tried to get in the house." Emilie informed him.

"She pulled on the front door and she pulled on the back door," Patton explained.

"She did it three times…" Emilie added.

"Well, there was no intent to try and do a criminal act; she just wanted to talk to you." .

This concerned me and must have worried Patton. How would the officer know what Andrea wanted?

"I would appreciate you not telling what's going on with the physical thing because she (Andrea) doesn't know yet. I don't want her going home and coaching her three-year-old not to say anything. The three-year-old already told her dad that she watched her hit Emilie the other day. That's why I haven't told Andrea why Emilie doesn't want to see her. CPS didn't get to talk to Andrea today; I guess they didn't make it over there."

"When's the last time your mom hit you?" The officer asked Emilie.

"Um, last Friday."

"How did she hit you?"

"She slapped me in the face, well she didn't slap. She grabbed and scratched me…" Emilie began.

120

"How did she grab you?"

"She grabbed me. She said I had an attitude and told me to go for a run. She just grabbed me real quick and said she had to tell me something and her nail caught on my skin and scratched me. I don't really what happened but she grabbed me and scratched me. I had scratches right there and a scratch right there." Emilie pointed to her cheek and neck where the scratches had been six days earlier.

"Okay, let me go talk to her, we'll be back in a minute, okay?" He said while leaving the doorway and walking through our front courtyard.

"Thank you." Patton closed the door.

Nearly an hour later, I suggested to my husband that he check with the officers to see if they could take their conversation with Andrea elsewhere. Multiple police vehicles had been in front of our home for almost an hour.

A few minutes later, he went outside, but just sat on the chair in the courtyard keeping a watchful eye. The police re-emerged up the walkway and immediately blocked the door to our home. They explained to my husband that he had two choices: "give the child to the mother. or go to jail."

When my husband challenged them by saying they had no right to send a reportedly abused child back to the care of the abuser, they repeated the two choices. Patton told them he was going to speak to his wife and children. As he lifted his hand to the doorknob, the big brutish officer, Michael Thacker, handcuffed him against the wall outside of our door. My husband was getting arrested!

Patton yelled out each of our names, "Lisa! Emilie! McKenna!"

The loudness of his voice startled Emilie and me. As a distraction, we had been playing cards in our safe haven, the corner of my bedroom. We raced to the door and saw Patton being handcuffed and pressed hard against the wall next to our mailbox. Officer Thacker kept repeating, "Stop resisting! Stop resisting!" He was in handcuffs and facing the wall, there was no resisting. Patton was shouting, "I'm NOT resisting! I didn't do anything!" repeatedly.

I was careful to stay in our house with the door wide open with McKenna who had arrived there first, and my stepdaughter. Both were crying hysterically which was saying something since Emilie had been so tough on the exterior.

She cried out. "Why are you arresting MY DAD? You should be arresting MY MOM! HE didn't do anything!" I remained as calm and strong as I could but was likely in shock.

Couldn't the law protect my husband while he protected his own child? It felt like a horrible movie and a nightmare all combined into one. I didn't know what to say or do!

Officer Thacker then threatened to arrest me too if *I* didn't give up my stepdaughter! It was surreal. We were all confused and the girls were crying hysterically. I didn't know what to say except to rationalize the law which my husband had conveyed earlier.

"But you can't come into my home and take anyone without a warrant. How can you want my stepdaughter to go with her abusive mother? There is an open investigation of the abuse; it has been reported! This isn't fair!" I cried.

The bully Thacker told me that the injunction was denied and repeated that he would arrest me too and the children would go into protective custody. They told me I had two minutes to decide.

While the front door was wide open (I wasn't sure if I was allowed to close it I just knew that they couldn't come in) I told them to wait a minute that I had to make a phone call. I grabbed my husband's cell phone and called my husband's best friend, Jim, who was a criminal defense attorney. Jim was at our door within five minutes.

It was past midnight when the police finally reached the child welfare authorities. The police and the DCF negotiated an agreement to release my stepdaughter to another party as long as the mother approved. So they agreed that Emilie didn't have to go with Andrea because of what DCF said but they wouldn't allow Patton to have her now that they knew she needed to be away from her? This made no sense! They even called into the car where my husband was handcuffed and asked Patton where Emilie should go. This was a circus! The St. Petersburg Police Department was a mess. Patton said that Jim could take her to his house. They told him that Andrea wouldn't agree to Jim but Andrea did approve Emilie going with Diane. Of course she had, it was her next door neighbor and this also meant Emilie would be leaving in the same car with Andrea.

Jim came into the house and somehow stood calmly, while reassuring me it would be okay. I so appreciated his strength as I had no time to pray and felt absolutely hopeless. I felt I had no choice as one of the other police officers, the slender young man, reiterated that if I were to keep my stepdaughter, I would be subject to arrest for interference of visitation. The threat by two officers lead me to believe they actually knew what they were saying, but they were wrong, (as I later discovered in the 787.03 statute.)

My husband was one of the most respected, loved, and honest of people I had ever known and now *he* was going to jail? How had Andrea turned this around? What power did she have? The law was once again enabling a very unstable parent to continue with her malice and even assisting her in her vendetta against her child's father.

Reluctantly, I helped my stepdaughter pack a bag to take to Andrea's neighbor's house and reminded her that she didn't owe her mother a single word or explanation or have to answer any of her questions. Jim, standing by my side reiterated that she didn't have to talk to her at all in the car, if she didn't want to. Emilie was so devastated, and powerless. Her face was pale and distraught. She looked to be almost in a daze in her eyes. I think she was in shock on some level. She was worried that her mom would come take her from Diane's house and asked what she should do? Jim told her that Diane promised the police she would keep her safe at her house for the night and she would look out for her.

I was dying on the inside feeling her pain. Emilie couldn't stop asking if her dad was going to be okay. Jim was speaking with the officers outside but continued to come into Emilie's room every couple of minutes for support. He assured Emilie that her dad would be okay and out on bond in just a few short hours. It was reassuring to me that my husband had a friend so dedicated to helping him; I knew Jim would take care of this whole mess.

I gave Emilie a huge hug and told her how much I loved her and how brave she was. I cried as she left, making the police promise that my stepdaughter wouldn't have to say a word to her mother and that she wouldn't even be in the same seat of the car. They verbally obliged and I trusted them but I was unable to see her enter the car and where she was seated since Diane's car was parked out of view from my front door. I didn't dare walk outside, since I felt they might trick me into some sort of arrest. I didn't trust the St. Petersburg Police Department, how could I after they just arrested an innocent man and left a child abuser once again, empowered, free, and with no consequences. My body was trembling all over and I felt physically sick. Fear had raced through my nerves as I tried to process everything that had just happened.

I insisted on pressing charges on the attempted break in so the slim younger officer stayed behind to allow me to file a report. He seemed to have softened a little. "For what it's worth, I believed that your stepdaughter was telling the truth about her mom but we had no choice."

Six hours later, after having his mug shot taken and uploaded on the Internet for the world to see, being finger-printed, suffering the humiliation of being strip searched and having to spread his naked buttocks, then finally being placed in a "pod" at the county jail, my husband was released on bond.

With both of us being completely sleep deprived, I was surprised we were able to talk so deeply and lengthy, but adrenaline will do that to you. Patton told me how Officer Thacker after having arrested him and putting him in the car found out that there was an open investigation with DCF on Andrea and one of the other officers asked him, "Should we release him?" Officer Thacker answered him, "No, he's an attorney, he'll sue me".

The police were morally wrong to force my stepdaughter to be in the presence of her mother, but their ignorance of Florida law was truly a disappointment.

My husband experienced and reported domestic violence against his former wife during their marriage. He knew what she was capable of. The second clause specifically states that "the defendant had reasonable cause..." which allows the defendant his own interpretation of danger. If my husband didn't believe that his daughter was in danger, he would not have filed the report with CPS or all of the motions early that morning.

It is time for our judges and law enforcement to *know* these guidelines and the entire Chapter 787 from the Florida Legislator Statutes.

The only choice my husband and I had at this point was to worry about Emilie and await the formal injunction hearing almost two weeks later. It took our own prodding through the investigation's social worker who visited our home to interview Emilie to learn any information regarding Emilie's safety and whereabouts. The social worker, Janice, had met with Emilie at Diane's house and spoken with her for a few minutes the day after the arrest before taking my stepdaughter to her mother's house and talking with her in front of Andrea! Janice reassured Patton that Emilie was safe at Andrea's house for the weekend and that she counseled Andrea for a couple of hours. She also mentioned that Andrea had to sign an agreement to not touch Emilie or Sarah except to give her affectionate hugs.

She said, "The mother is fully aware that Emilie may contact the police if she feels she is in danger and that she may go to the neighbors if she must to do so." Patton was devastated. How could they think that two hours of counseling and a signed "contract" would spare Emilie of any physical abuse or mental anguish? No child should be allowed to dwell with an abuser, particularly when Andrea was now also going to be getting in-home counseling two or three days a week during their investigation. It was particularly disturbing since Andrea's public records verified a lengthy history of making false allegations against her daughter's respective fathers. How could any officials who are hired to protect children not see through Andrea? Her alienation made their custody dispute one of the lengthiest on record of Pinellas County.

While awaiting the hearing, we learned of the judge's verdict in George's trial. George received 35% visitation. If only our legislation enacted a 50/50 time-sharing rule at the onset of all custodial agreements, I wonder how many children could be spared from this malicious abuse. Why were mothers awarded a majority of time in most cases? This made no sense at all. We have long passed the fifties, when women were often stay-at-home mothers. Most families of this generation had both the parents in the work force. Shouldn't both parents have equal time-sharing?

Following that long weekend where Emilie was subjected to stay at her mother's house, we were anxious to hear from Emilie herself on Monday, when Patton's scheduled visitation came. Emilie told us about the car ride. She said that she didn't say one word to her mother in the car and that her mother asked her only once during the ride, "Why are you telling people lies about me?"

Emilie told me, "I remembered you telling me, Lisa, that I didn't have to answer any of my mom's questions and I just ignored her. I was scared to even talk to her. She was in the back seat with my little sister on the drive over. I said good night to Sarah and went right away into Diane's house." The fact that Sarah was present for all of this was unknown to me at that point. That meant she actually witnessed all of the antics, three lit up police vehicles, and her mother playing the victim until she got her way.

Patton asked if Andrea tried to come into Diane's house. Emilie said she did, but Diane told her "no" that she "was going to do what the officers told her to do and keep Emilie without any interference" from Andrea.

Emilie continued. "But the next day Janice came and talked to me for a little bit. I had already told Diane and her son (he was twenty-four) that night I stayed with them, the truth about my mom and what she had been making me do and lie about since I was little. I was glad that they at least believed me because Diane's son said he used to hear my mom scream and cuss at me all the time through his bedroom window."

Patton lowered his head in sadness hearing his daughter's new found bravado to speak up against her mother even to people her mother had convinced were allies. "Honey, I am really proud of you, I know how hard all this is to talk about and I am so sorry I couldn't protect you."

"But dad, you had to go to jail! I can't believe you got arrested! Why won't anyone do anything about my mom? Why does she get away with everything and you go to jail for protecting me?" There it was, the elusive question for which no one could answer.

Emilie's sympathy warmed Patton's heart as he hugged her. She asked him what it was like and after he told her how the booking process went he resumed his concern for her time at Andrea's.

"Honey, was your mom nice to you this weekend?"

"I mean yeah, I guess so but she is just trying to act nice so I don't say anything more. And she kept calling me a liar at first! She kind of stopped when I reminded her that she wasn't supposed to talk to me about any of the court stuff 'cause the social worker told her not to.'"

Patton reminded Emilie that she would see him again on Wednesday that week and then Friday was his weekend with her. The following weekend of June 21st, was his weekend and rather than returning her that Sunday at eight o'clock, he would begin his one week vacation with her. Patton feared Emilie spending too much time with her mother before the hearing would give Andrea more time to reprogram his daughter and/or get her too frightened to testify.

The hearing finally came during that "vacation" week on Thursday, June 27, 2013. Our family was reinvigorated and ready to go. Emilie had already been with us since the preceding Friday so she was very anxious to speak to the Judge. Here was yet another new judge, we'll call this one Judge C.

McKenna, Emilie and I entered the court room just as Andrea's attorney began his opening. Patton, his attorney, Scott, and his friend, Jim were in the courtroom. Andrea's attorney came right out of the gate with the fact that my husband was arrested and out on bond. He didn't say for what reason but rather referred to him more or less as a criminal to capture Judge C's attention, I suppose.

"Look at my mom," Emilie whispered to me as we sat in the gallery of the courtroom. "She is so phony. Why is she up there fake crying; she is so fake." This was not what I expected to hear from my stepdaughter since over the years she feared her so much and I was accustomed to her *not* berating her character, but usually defending her. Not today. Emilie was confident, she had a voice today and was ready to be heard. Andrea was standing at the podium with her attorney, trembling and looking frail like an old lady. Her hair was up and in a haphazard bun. She was wearing the familiar conservative navy suit she had worn at several hearings years earlier. It did seem to bring her luck in the past.

When Emilie went in chambers with the judge, she met with him for just less than fifteen minutes. A few months later we received a transcript of this meeting which bore out what Emilie told us.

After some brief small talk, the judge began his questions. I have done some minor editing to keep it short and readable.

Judge: "Sometimes when parents are divorced, they don't always agree on everything. There's a little disagreement here. There's some talk about perhaps you've had some injuries that resulted when you were over at your mom's house."

Emilie: "Yes."

Judge: "And have you gotten injured over at your mom's house?"

Emilie: "Yes, plenty of times."

Judge: "All right. Well, explain to me what's happened over there."

Emilie: "She has pinched my tongue before. She has long acrylic nails. When I was about eight or nine, she would pinch my tongue to like, get me to be quiet, really hard. She has given me, I think three black eyes. She has given me scratches on my face. The last day of school with my final exam I had scratches on my face. I'm really upset because... I mean, she tells me to call her right after the final exam is over. So you know I'm like crying at school because I have scratches all over me and everybody is asking me what is wrong, you know, what happened and stuff. And I'm like, "Well, my little sister just scratched me by accident," because (Mom) tells me to lie to people. She tells me all the time. She's like, "You better tell people that your little sister Sarah did it." And she's three. You know, so she... I've had to lie about two black eyes, saying that my little sister kicked me in the face.

"So you know, it's just I'm way... I'm really scared to go over there. I mean, I'm constantly getting in trouble for things that I don't even do. And when she finds out that I actually stood up and told people the truth, then I am really going to get in trouble.

"So, I mean, it's... there's been some other things that have happened, like I've had wrist issues. I have tendonitis in this wrist. And I remember it started when she hit my wrist, and it like popped. That's when it really started hurting. And it still – it's been ongoing for about two years. So it's hard for me to golf. It's just really interfering with everything that I do.

"But it's really hard for me to say anything that she doesn't agree with. She just goes off on me..."

Judge: "All right. Explain to me how you got the scratches."

Emilie: "I go for a run and she made me come back inside. She was on the phone with my dad I remember. She started acting like she wasn't mad at me. She said I had an attitude—I was really overwhelmed—I mean, she says I'm allowed to have five minutes in the bathroom to brush my teeth, get dressed, floss, do all this other stuff and she tells me I'm not allowed to wash my face. After that she's like, 'Come clean the cat box' and then she is telling me to go back in the bathroom. I was like, 'Okay mom, I am really overwhelmed right now.' She's like, 'okay go for a run.' She brought me back in. You know, she's on the phone with my dad, acting like she's not mad at me and I was like, 'Mom, why are you acting like you're not mad at me all of a sudden, because you're on the phone with my dad?' That set her off. So she brought me in my room and started hitting me. And then she lied right in front of the CPI investigator, saying that she did not hit me."

Judge: "Explain to me how it was that she hit you. What did she do exactly?"

Emilie: "She scratched me; she went like this. And it left marks."

Judge: On your neck?

Emilie: Yes. And I had acrylic nails at that time. I ended up ripping one off when I was in there, in that fight.

I mean, I didn't do anything. I had to just sit there and I wasn't allowed to talk because then she hits me again and [I'm afraid] she'll give me another black eye."

Judge: "When was the last time you got a black eye?"

Emilie: "Right before I went to Aspen. I think it was...its June right now. I think it was during March.

"There was also a time, I think the day before my dad got me and she just went off. She started driving like 110 miles an hour in her Beemer. I have to sit in the front and my little sister is in the back seat and is like, 'Slow down, slow down.' I was like, 'Mom, you really need to slow down because you are going like 110 miles an hour.' I was looking at the MPH meter, whatever it's called...speedometer. I was looking at it the entire time. It was 110. And then she almost ran into like three people."

Judge: "How often is there an incident where you get scratched or hurt or something?"

Emilie: Probably about you know, once a week. But I mean sometimes she hits me and she doesn't leave a mark. I mean, this has pretty much been going on my whole life... And she's given me a fat lip before. You might be able to still see it. It's a little bit like a dent or a mark."

Judge: This happened pretty recently?

Emilie: About six months ago... well, actually probably about a year ago. But it's still there, the mark is still there."

Judge: "Does she mostly hit you in the face?"

Emilie: "Yes sir. I mean this whole wrist issue; she tries to blame it on golf. She tries to put makeup on my black eye. She tries to put like Neosporin on my scratches. And you know, she tries to act like my little sister did everything. And I feel bad for my little sister because she's getting blamed for everything that she didn't do."

Judge: "How old is she?"

Emilie: "She's three."

Judge: "And how did you hurt your wrist?"

Emilie: "She smacked my wrist and it popped. And it went back and forward. I'm not exactly sure, but it popped out. I had to get physical therapy for about five months. My mom agreed to do it because she just lied and said it had to do with golf."

Judge: "Did you get an MRI on the wrist?"

Emilie: "I had to get a CAT scan. They put me in a cast; it was a splint, a brace – a cast thing."

They talked a bit further about the family, who lives with whom, Patton, McKenna, me, Sarah, etc. Then Emilie added that her mom locked her out of the house with her little sister in the back yard and that Andrea made her watch her little sister at the park or McDonald's while she was on the phone talking about things that had happened with her ex-boyfriend.

Emilie: "She gets away with everything. I was trying to defend myself once and she totally acted like I didn't break my acrylic nail which really hurt. It almost rips off your nail. That hurts. And then she acted like she didn't give me the black eye or scratches in front of the investigator. I think she believed it. She ended up signing a paper; I had to sign it too that first day after my dad was arrested when I went to stay at my mom's neighbors because the police made me go. The social worker took me to my mom's that next day and that is when we both signed the contract. It said that there will be no physical contact with either my sister or me. And then my mom started to say, 'Well, I wasn't! I wasn't! Does this mean I can still go like this?' (Emilie gestured to mimic her mother putting her hand on Emilie's mouth) Because that's all she says she ever does. And [the DCF investigator] was like, 'No. You cannot have any physical contact unless you want to hug or kiss your child.' The next day [my mom] said, 'You know, I could still go like this.' I was like 'No, you can't you signed something. I signed it too.' She's acting like she never signed anything."

Judge: "She puts her hand over your mouth?"

Emilie: "She says that's the only physical contact that she ever has."

Judge: "Why does she put her hand over your mouth?"

Emilie: "Because she says I'm too loud and I can't, I mean I'm not even loud. I'm trying to explain why I'm upset and I'm overwhelmed and she's like 'You need to just shut up.' And then she cusses. She is constantly cussing at me, constantly swearing. I go to school upset all the time. I mean the last day of school I should be able to enjoy myself with all my friends. But I'm like crying, like the entire day. And everybody is asking me what's wrong, what's wrong. I was like, 'I can't talk about it.' And they're like, 'come on.' So it's just affecting my friendships and it's just affecting everything in my life. I'm so tired of just dealing with it."

A few minutes after this interview, we were all in the courtroom to see if the judge would grant the restraining order for my stepdaughter against her mother.

The judge ruled. "I'm going to find at this point the burden by the petitioner (Patton and Emilie) has not been met so I'm going to deny the petition for domestic violence." Was there any justice in our family law courts?

He ordered that the regular visitation to remain "as previously ordered" and that they all attend family counseling. He did however, grant my husband's motion to appoint a Guardian Ad Litem. Emilie would be going back to her mother's when my husband's "vacation visitation" was over that Sunday.

I have rarely, if ever, seen my husband as speechless and angry as he was that day. My stepdaughter and he never felt more beaten down and defeated. After learning what was said privately in chambers between the judge and Emilie one could only surmise that perhaps the judge didn't take the time to see all the unfounded abuse allegations Andrea made of Patton and try to see if perhaps he should inquire about alienation. False abuse reporting, although a felony, is very common in cases of parental

133

alienation, yet remains unpunished. Alienation is child abuse. Andrea got away with both.

Another judge's ruling once again signed off on Andrea's ability to physically and emotionally abuse my stepdaughter and the worst was still yet to come.

We tried to make the most of the little time left with Emilie before she returned home to Andrea. Emilie was so happy at our home, so relaxed and comfortable until the day she had to go back. Her courage and candor to finally share with Child Protective Services, three police officers, and a Pinellas County Judge were completely futile. Nobody would help this innocent child victim break free from her mother's imprisonment, nobody cared.

About fifteen minutes after my husband dropped Emilie off on Sunday, he received an email from Andrea. She was beginning *her* one-week vacation with Emilie that day at 8 p.m., until the following Sunday at the same time. That meant Emilie had all those consecutive days with Andrea but not an ounce of support or protection from her. We prayed that Andrea would be extra kind to Emilie since she was still under investigation and was receiving home counseling services with CPS, but we had no idea.

Following those long, harrowing days, Emilie arrived at the bank drop-off for her Monday night visitation with Patton from five-thirty until eight that evening. The first hour was brutal. Emilie had digressed right back to the secretive, moody child she was prior to her admission of her mother's abuse. Patton and I both had sinking feelings in our stomachs. I gently asked if there was anything that we should know that was happening at her mom's.

I was surprised Emilie quickly had an answer. "I called my friend Jessica from my mom's house and told her everything my mom had been doing—how she was abusing me and everything. My mom must have overheard some of my conversation with her so she made me call back and lie to Jessica." Emilie clammed up when we asked her about the lie. "I don't want to talk about it." She digressed.

"Right, I understand, and I'm not trying to be nosy but as long as it wasn't lies about Dad. She just wanted you to tell Jessica that what you had just told her about your mom was lies, right?" I asked delicately.

"No, she wanted me to call and tell Jessica that Dad was arrested and that he hurt my wrist and that is why I had to keep going to the doctor's for my wrist."

"Honey, it's okay, you told the truth about the arrest which is public record anyway. Daddy isn't ashamed of his arrest because he did it to defend your safety against your mom. Don't worry about that. It even says on the police website with his mug shot, 'interference with custody.' But, your mom made you say it was because he hurt your wrist? That is not okay; that is daddy's reputation that is being destroyed. Jessica may have told her parents and now they may think badly of Daddy when it was your mom who physically abuses you. That is wrong and unfair to Dad, don't you think?" I asked squarely. I had a way of getting Emilie to open up to me. I'm not sure of why but I like to think it was because she trusted me and that she knew I truly cared about her and justice for her and Patton.

"Yes, but my mom was standing right there while I called her!" Emilie sounded defeated like there had been no option.

I wanted to offer a solution that would not only do right by Patton but also take some of Emilie's guilt or shame away about what her mother made her do. "Well honey, I know you have texted Jessica from daddy's phone, would you like to call her and explain the truth to her?"

"No, but I do want to text her." Emilie turned to Patton, who had been listening to our exchange, and asked if she could use his phone. She then she went into our bedroom, propped herself onto her elbows while lying on her stomach and typed a text message to her friend. She said she didn't want to be interrupted. She was very serious about it.

135

After she came out of our bedroom, she handed the phone to her dad. Patton asked if she deleted the text after sending it or if he could read it. She said yes, he could read it:

Hey, just wanted to let you know that what I said about my dad was a lie. If u noticed, I got really awkward on the phone because my mom heard everything I told u about her. The only thing that was true about my dad was that he got arrested for trying to protect me from my mom because my mom hits me. He never hit me, my mom told me to lie to u about him. Everything I told u about my mom is true and there are a lot more bad things about my mom that I didn't tell u. I am very sorry for involving u in this situation...I can tell you more about my situation when we get back in school. (If you want me to.) Again I am very sorry.

Patton thanked her for doing the right thing and said he was so sorry that he couldn't protect her. He took the tender moment to ask Emilie if anything had happened over the last week with her mom. Emilie said that her mother put her hand over Emilie's mouth if she got mad about her attitude or something she said but she didn't directly hit her. Sounding bitter, she said that counselors were there and her mother had lied right in front of them denying any abuse.

I tried to encourage Emilie by reminding her that all of this wasn't over.

"Yeah but no one will ever do anything about her, she just keeps getting away with everything!" She sounded exhausted.

I had to give her hope. I wanted her to have faith that one day someone will get it, they will understand. "Emilie, there is an open investigation on her, do you realize that? Don't give up! The truth will come out eventually, and she will be stopped. In the meantime, if she lays a finger on you, you run, you leave, you defend yourself! You are two inches taller than she and a whole lot stronger; don't let her scare you!" I said emphatically.

"Wait, there is still an investigation on my mom?" She asked with hope.

"Absolutely, this is not over!" I reiterated.

"Oh, I didn't know! I thought it was done since she has me back." Emilie explained.

Patton shook his head. "No honey, this is all still getting looked into. You don't need to worry about that, you just make sure if she ever hits or makes a mark on you, you report it, call 911, or run to a neighbor's if you have to."

"My mom doesn't let me out of her sight. I can't do anything. Nobody believes me anyway or will do anything!"

She was right, nobody would do anything. This was a travesty of justice and the safety of two little innocent girls was being compromised.

"Honey, stay strong and know that I am doing everything I can legally do to get your mom to stop hitting you so she can get some help. I am disappointed too, but I will never give up." Patton hugged her as they left to go to the car for her drop off at the bank.

Emilie was always ready for a round of golf even on vacation!

These are grumblers, malcontents, following their own sinful desires; they are loud-mouthed boasters, showing favoritism to gain advantage.
Jude 1:16 NIV

XVIII: Liars and Hypocrites

There was only one more visit from Emilie after that because Andrea had begun to withhold her from Patton. For forty-two consecutive days, Patton didn't see his daughter. Getting through those weeks was one of the most torturous tribulations of his life. He had no way to ascertain the well-being of his daughter and he certainly had no way to protect her.

Patton called the police each and every day of missed visitation, and yes, the police went to Andrea's house to complete a report several times but what the authorities weren't doing was stopping her.

The police continuously said, call after call, day after day, report after report, that it wasn't a criminal matter but a civil one. What hypocrites! Our police department clearly had double standards with regard to parental rights, visitation, and blatant criminal misconduct.

We prayed to God, over and over for justice, but we prayed far more for the safety and well-being of Emilie and now, her little three-year-old sister, Sarah.

The Monday that followed one of Patton's earlier visitation deprived weekends, an officer came to our house.

In the brief time between when I noticed the patrol car out front and actually opened the door, I felt a sense of euphoria. Had Andrea finally been arrested for being in contempt of the visitation agreement which the judge had clearly stated was to be abided? Did the police finally close their investigation of all her false abuse allegations against Patton and George, and arrest her for that? My optimism waned quickly.

I opened the door to a very large black gentleman whose size alone was intimidating. He had an unpleasant expression when he told me the reason for his visit was that Andrea called them to tell them that *Patton* was under investigation for emotional child abuse and that was why she had been withholding the visits he had been reporting.

I was dumbfounded. Andrea had added that Patton had called and "threatened" her. She apparently showed her caller ID which showed he had called her two days prior. There was no message; the call never connected, just rang and rang as he tried to speak with his daughter during his legal visitation time that Andrea was keeping Emilie from him.

I told the officer that Andrea had been withholding visitation illegally and that *she* was the one under investigation for physical child abuse! I explained that she was receiving in-home counseling from DCF three days a week. The officer looked confused and seemed agitated. I didn't know what it was that seemed to rub him the wrong way, that Andrea lied to him or that he thought I might be lying but he looked like he was about to roll his eyes as his mouth made a gesture of disgust. I asked him to wait for a moment while I got Patton on speaker phone at his office.

Patton reiterated what I said and added the report number for the DCF case against Andrea along with the contact information for the Pinellas Sheriff who was in charge of the investigation. He also provided the many police report numbers for the withheld visitations thusfar. The officer proceeded to his car saying that he would check all the report numbers out. "If she lied to me, she is not going to get what she wants to get from my report." That was it? I was puzzled, why wouldn't he go arrest her for making a false police report and kidnapping her daughter. These were felonies!

Several hours later, around dinnertime that night the same officer came back to our home and this time Patton was there. The officer verified on my husband's phone (and the phone records that were on-line) that Patton's call never connected. Thus, the "threat" Andrea claimed, had to be false. He also verbally acknowledged that since this was in fact a Monday, Patton's day, he was witness that the child was being withheld again.

What happened? Nothing! Per usual, Andrea got away unscathed. Once again, our justice system let us down.

A few days later, Patton was as shocked when I checked public records and told him that Andrea filed a motion for an injunction/restraining order against him that very morning! I explained that it said "denied" in the status, so that was good. But he went to the court house a few hours later to get a copy and was told the disposition of her request was still pending.

Apparently, Andrea had gone to the Clearwater courthouse for her restraining order the day before. When she learned that it was denied due to "no imminent threat" she court shopped! She went to the St. Petersburg court house and filled out another request. Because she knew the reason for denial, she fabricated several detailed threats on her life by Patton. She withheld that *she* was under investigation and counseling by DCF. She didn't mention that she had attempted a restraining order the prior day and that it was denied. On her first request, she never once mentioned a single threat made by Patton.

On the second request, she used a different last name, a hyphenated maiden-marital version of her name to no doubt conceal from the court that she had attempted a request the day prior. The Clearwater courthouse made a clerical error by not flagging the initial request, so the St. Petersburg courthouse had no reason to suspect foul play. Based on the words "threatened to kill me" used not once or twice, but *four* times on her new request, the St. Petersburg judge had no choice but to grant the restraining order temporarily that day until a hearing date was set.

Once again, Andrea's false allegations meant Patton would no longer be able to see his daughter or make any attempt to communicate with her until after the hearing. The police never arrested Andrea for perjury regarding her police report, they never arrested her for the several counts of contempt in the court ordered visitation, or kidnapping. No, instead, this child-abusing criminal was granted a temporary restraining order against the only stable parent Emilie had.

There was no justice in Pinellas County.

I was quickly losing hope for Emilie's welfare. I am a proud Christian woman and I don't believe in luck, but I kept thinking "you reap what you sow," from the Bible and wondered if God's answer had to be riddled with such cataclysms to get to the best solution. We had no choice but to remain faithful to Him. He had this, I kept telling myself over and over. Patton could do nothing do but once again, wait for the hearing. But, as Murphy's Law seemed to dominate this whole mess, it got worse yet again.

About ten days into his restraining order, Patton went to play golf and while in his cart, he finished a phone call he made to his friend, Jim. After that, he inadvertently butt-dialed our home. I was out of the house most of the day and didn't know but McKenna answered and kept saying "Dad? Dad? Are you there?"

When I got home, I answered a knock on the door and discovered a pair of police officers. The same officer that Andrea lied to two weeks earlier stood with the female who was there the night of the arrest; both looked serious. "Is Mr. Young here?" He asked me.

"No, he is golfing or maybe at the grocery store by now." I answered politely.

"Do you know when he will be back?"

"No, but probably not too long." I responded with a little confusion.

"We need to speak with him. He is currently under an injunction with no contact and he called his ex-wife." He informed me.

"Oh my goodness, I can't believe that, He is an attorney and knows better. He had to have butt or pocket dialed her. He does that to me all the time." I half chuckled.

"Well, he can explain that to the state's attorney, then." He said stoically.

"Okay, but you need to see his phone; I am sure he wouldn't call her. He gave up calling her because she never picked up the calls or like she did before, lie and say he called and said something that he didn't. I am telling you, he wouldn't do that." I begged for them to hear him out.

"Well, he should have deleted her number from his phone or put a lock screen on so he wouldn't do that. Like I said he can explain it to the judge." He reiterated. Then the mousy female officer spoke up condescendingly said, "that would be the very first thing I would do, delete her number from my contact list."

"I understand that, but my husband isn't a police officer and that number is the only number he has to reach his daughter. I would never think of deleting it either, quite frankly." I was agitated that they had been so rude especially given that Andrea had just lied to this same man about a week prior when she said Patton was being investigated and now they wanted to tell me how stupid my husband was?

When Patton arrived home about a half hour later, they looked at his phone to see several consecutive calls within the course of a minute, none of them to Andrea's number. They didn't seem to care; they arrested Patton again.

This was a living nightmare.

In the arraignment hearing the following morning around 9 o'clock, the judge admonished Patton for the accidental dialing, informing him again that he should have deleted Andrea's number from his phone. However, I had gone to the Clearwater courthouse a few days before to ask them about Andrea's dual filing with another courthouse in the same county. That is where I learned of

142

the "clerical error" and Patton was now armed with my file of both of Andrea's injunction requests. Patton's attorney informed the judge that there never should have been a restraining order granted to Andrea in the first place because of the court-shopping and the perjury regarding the threats.

The judge verbally admonished Andrea while she spewed crocodile tears saying how fearful she was of him. It wasn't convincing enough to keep my husband in custody.

Even though Patton was still technically out on bond, the judge released him, thank God. Finally, a proper ruling.

Although, this second arrest wouldn't look good in his upcoming hearing to have his temporary restraining order dismissed, the judge made it clear that perjury and court shopping would not be tolerated.

When the hearing came three days later, Patton; his new criminal defense attorney, Bill; and his friend Jim, along with Patton's brother, McKenna, and I, all convened in the court room to defend my husband. Sarah's father, George, as well as Andrea's next door neighbor's son, Joe, who heard Andrea's persistent expletives and yelling at her daughters, were also there to support Patton. Emilie was not there as this was during those six weeks that Andrea was withholding visitation from Patton.

Who was there for Andrea? No one but a "victim's advocate" from Safe Start who clearly had no idea of the liar Andrea was.

The judge from the onset said there would be a slight delay and asked if there was any way the two parties could work it out during their wait. After nearly an hour of Andrea objecting to "willfully dropping" her injunction motion, her attorneys must have convinced her that if the judge saw the two completely conflicting reports that she filed within a day of each other, she might be convicted of a felony, so she agreed. She signed and verbally agreed to drop her motion. The judge told the parties that he was glad that she had because if that case had come to him, it would have had a different outcome. He also ordered a no-contact order between the parties except for email and neither parent could call the other to speak to the child, email only.

So now this chapter was over but there was plenty more to come.

Patton had missed out of most of Emilie's summer break so after more than forty days, he was beyond excited to see her again the following Monday, his last legal visitation date of the summer. But Andrea didn't bring Emilie to the bank for drop-off yet again!

Two days later, Emilie started the eighth grade. Patton hoped that he would have no conflict picking her up from school as he was legally permitted to do. When Emilie emerged from the school building, she greeted her dad with a confused and angry look, with words to match. "Dad, what are you doing here? You're not supposed to be here." Obviously, Andrea had brainwashed Emilie over the summer as we knew she would.

"What are you talking about? Who said I'm not supposed to be here?" Patton asked with a heavy heart.

"Everybody. I'm supposed to go home with my mom. She told me I am or I will get in trouble."

Just as she answered, the principal came over and said, "Well, I have two parents here to pick up Emilie. Who are you going with?"

"Where is my mom?" Emilie asked.

"She is in the parking lot, in the car line," he told her.

"Honey, I don't want you to get in trouble and have problems with your mom, but this is *my* visitation and I miss seeing you!" Patton was hurt.

"I know but I'm going to get in trouble."

"Who are you going with, Emilie?" The principal repeated.

After Emilie's long pause and confused expression, Patton submitted. "Fine honey, I don't want you to get in trouble with your mom so if you think that will happen, then just go."

She did.

Patton personally contacted the principal via email later that day to explain how things stood starting with the child abuse confessions from Emilie and all the legal actions that had occurred since. The principal admitted he had only heard Andrea's side of the story, and it was totally different, laden with threats and arrests. When Patton produced the police reports, the DCF investigation report numbers and contacts as well as the original MSA citing his legal rights, the principal vowed to research and verify all the information he had been given.

Patton showed up the following Monday to pick up Emilie from school except she was nowhere to be found. The principal was upset after he called several of her teachers in their classrooms and learned that Andrea came and took Emilie directly from class rather than signing her out and following protocol.

The principal contacted Andrea by phone and told her that if she were ever to remove the child again from the school without authorization, he would personally call the police on her. In fact, he told her not to come on campus unless it was her day to pick Emilie up from school.

With her usual disregard for authority, Andrea showed up that Monday anyway. The principal called the police.

When the police arrived, the officer wasted no time cutting to the chase. "Who has legal visitation today?"

"The father does," the principal answered.

"Fine, then go with your father." He said authoritatively to Emilie.

."But, you don't know what's going on! He's been arrested!" Andrea appealed. She just loved telling as many people she could that Patton had been arrested, it made him look like the villain.

"I know all I need to know. If the father has legal visitation, he is allowed to take his daughter. If you have a problem with that, you need to file a motion for the courts to change custody."

A policeman in our city with sense and ethics really did exist! Emilie's visitations were finally restored without further interference from Andrea.

The timing was good as Emilie was turning thirteen years old and we were throwing her a surprise party, the next Sunday, the day that preceded her birthday. It was a great party with about fifteen guests including Sarah, Andrea's parents, and George and his children. Emilie received the longed-for black Labrador we rescued from a shelter who she named, Jolie as a birthday present from Patton and me.

The next day, on Emilie's actual thirteenth birthday September 2nd, 2013, her mother gave her something even more memorable than Jolie. Andrea called the police on her!

Emilie told us she and her mother left the mall and Andrea was ranting on the car ride home. Emilie told her mother she just didn't want to live with her anymore and wanted to live with her father. Her mother became enraged and poked at Emilie's collarbone. Her collarbone could have withstood the pain, but the lymph node next to it, could not. Emilie took her mother's poked finger and pushed it away saying, "Stop mom, you're hurting me." That no touching contract was still in force and Andrea knew Emilie would be telling us or someone.

Andrea's fury grew. "Ow!" she squealed. "You hurt me! I am calling the police."

She did.

Poor Emilie celebrated her big day as a new teenager with a lecture from a policewoman about not pushing her mother around while Andrea continued crying and playing the victim.

Two more officers arrived and tried to calm the situation down by asking Emilie, "What can we do to help you?"

"Call my dad."

They said they "couldn't do that." Why not?

They were kind to my stepdaughter and quelled Andrea's emotional pleas while Emilie gave them another idea. "I don't care; you can take me away to Juvenile Detention, I don't care! I just want to be away from her. She is a liar and a fake and she gets away with everything!"

Less than a month later, Emilie's *school* called the police and DCF on Emilie.

Emilie had been cutting herself and was Baker Acted. The Baker Act is also known as the Florida Mental Health act. The Baker Act is Chapter 394, Part I, Florida Statutes. It provides legal procedures for mental health examination and treatment, including: voluntary admission, involuntary examination, involuntary inpatient placement (IIP), involuntary outpatient placement (IOP). It also regulates: Crisis stabilization units (CSUs) and short-term residential treatment facilities (SRTs).[11]

My stepdaughter was now on suicide watch.

Emilie was committed to the Personal Enrichment Mental Health Services (PEMHS) of Pinellas County for almost two weeks. Patton had no idea until Emilie's second day there and only found out from the court-appointed family counselor, *not* from Andrea. He immediately visited his daughter for the brief one hour she was allowed to have visitors. On his first visit he learned from Emilie that she had been "cutting" since summer when her mother kept her from her dad those forty-two days.

Concurrently, Irene, a Guardian Ad Litem (GAL) was finally appointed and able to meet Emilie just in time. She was a warm motherly woman with whom Emilie felt immediately comfortable. She was understanding and not at all pushy. Her genuine smile shone brightly at Emilie. Irene witnessed Andrea's visits at the facility with her daughter, first hand.

Andrea visited her daughter daily and each time would question her about what Emilie told the judges, the police, the counselors, and the GAL about her. She made Emilie feel worse about revealing the truth and continued to call her a liar. Andrea went so far as to tell Emilie that she "was done with [her] and you're not a daughter to me anymore."

It hurt badly enough that Emilie soon found things to cut her arms and legs up with while under the supposed supervision of the county's mental health center. Emilie continued to say she was suicidal for the duration of her stay. Just a few days after Emilie's confinement to the facility, infuriated by how Andrea continued to make his daughter feel unloved and worthless, Patton filed yet another emergency motion to remove Andrea's rights to visitation. The motion would coincide with Emilie's exit hearing that was the protocol to determine if a child should be released from PEMHS.

To our surprise, the judge ruled in favor of the (GAL) who agreed with Patton's motion. The judge agreed with Patton and Irene that Emilie's overnights should be given solely to Patton at least temporarily–all of her overnights. Emilie was finally in safe custody! The only thing that could alter the new custody arrangement was Andrea filing a motion to have it changed. But that would take months to happen, if at all. The hearing had been on the tenth day of Emilie's commitment. Following the ruling, we rushed to PEHMS to share the good news with Emilie. She was quickly released and sent home with Patton and me.

Emilie's transition to living with us wasn't easy, particularly in the beginning. She still had anxiety about the motion which included four-hour visits each Wednesday and seven hours every other Saturday and Sunday, to Andrea. Emilie didn't want to see her mother at all, ever again.

The GAL and family counselor listened to her concerns and vowed to step in if they needed to. After speaking with Emilie and seeing her fear about her mother's physical and emotional abuse coupled with the possibility of Andrea keeping her from her father again,

148

they agreed she wouldn't have to see her mother at all for any of those hours, if she wasn't ready to. Emilie was relieved and chose to have *no* visitation with Andrea. Finally, she had some control and influence over what her mother could *not* do to her.

Additionally, the no-contact order was still in force so Andrea technically wasn't allowed to attempt contact Emilie, unless it was via email. Andrea never did, and my stepdaughter's terror of her mother slowly began to dissipate.

Emilie returned to school with a more positive outlook. That early September, Patton told her that if she were to ever cut herself again, he would have no alternative but to get her the help she needed at a residential treatment facility. But habits are hard to break and Emilie was now a cutter. Emilie again gashed her legs so brutally that the school became concerned about the other children who knew of, or saw, her bloody cry for help. Just two days after returning to school, the school administrator called the police, and then called Patton to let him know. Emilie told the police she had cut again because she was now worried about her little sister Sarah left behind in Andrea's care. Patton let the officers know his intention to commit her to a private facility and they honored it which was unusual as they generally Baker Acted them automatically to the county facility where Emilie had initially gone.

My husband took Emilie to a psychiatric facility where she signed in voluntarily. After just three days, she was released but her school would not allow her back for a couple of months. Instead, she would be schooled electronically over the Internet. Patton didn't keep her in a residential facility against her will after those three days as he was fearful that she might resent him and that she truly might commit suicide if she was "sent away". I thought Emilie badly needed to be at an inpatient care facility for a decent period of time to get through the trauma from Andrea's physical abuse & emotional torture. I wanted her to learn proper coping skills. I didn't want to keep worrying and wondering what could or would happen to her.

While Patton went to work, I played a sort of baby-sitter role for the next two weeks keeping a pretty watchful eye on Emilie. She mostly just played games on her phone, watched TV, or shot baskets in our driveway. I tried keeping her busy with shopping, playing checkers or cooking, but she was clearly bored. Her virtual schooling was delayed due to short staffing of the Pinellas County School Board and she needed to have something productive to do.

Each day, I checked Emilie's count of how long she had gone without cutting. I told her how proud of her I was for controlling the urge. I high-fived her with pride as I felt she needed the positive reinforcement. On the fourteenth day, she and I went through some cookbooks and I asked her to pick out a new recipe she would like to make and I would do the same. When we went to the grocery store to get the ingredients she stopped and looked at me with a small smile. "You know, Lisa, I probably spend more time with you than anyone else." She said.

"I know, I'm sorry but Dad has to work and fortunately, I don't." I said feeling badly for her.

"No, I'm not complaining. I just was saying that because I feel like we are always spending time together." She reassured me.

"Well, I don't mind. We have been getting along so well for so long, and I enjoy it." I told her. I could tell by her appreciative words and body language how awkward she felt expressing an honest connection or emotion toward a maternal figure. Emilie wasn't the warm and cuddly type, her mother prohibited it and never showed her the love that could come from a warm, secure hug. We never gave up though, she was getting hugs from Patton and me every day she was with us.

"Me too. I just wish I could see some of my friends from school," she said sadly.

When we got home from grocery shopping, I unloaded our wares and tidied up the house a bit. I was working in Emilie's room when the phone rang. Emilie answered and began speaking with her dad. Just as their conversation started, I ran out to grab an extension phone to share my shocking find.

"Patton, I was just in Emilie's room and I found a new blade!" I extended my hand outward. "Did you cut, Emilie?"

With Patton still on the phone to her ear and me in front of her with the other phone, she answered. "Yes."

"When, when did you do this?" He asked.

"Earlier, when we finished looking up recipes. I was bored." It seemed the abuse and alienation from her mother that caused the cutting had definitively become a habit. This was horrible.

I was especially disheartened that she told me that she got the blade from one of my cookbook sensors. Over the phone, Patton instructed her to show me where she cut herself.

She lifted her long basketball shorts leg up to reveal the word "FAT" inscribed on her upper thigh. I couldn't believe it. Why? Boredom? How sad, she certainly wasn't fat but she had very little self-esteem from the trauma of her mother's abuse to not being welcomed back to school. I felt completely discouraged so I could only imagine how Patton felt.

Emilie looked disappointed or perhaps even guilty but didn't really express much emotion. Patton came home from the office shortly after. He reiterated, yet again, that he had to get her into a facility but she promised to tell one of us if the urge presented itself, and that we could trust her. Addictions needed special attention. I didn't trust that Patton and I had the skillset or tools to remedy her problem. I also didn't trust Emilie as she had made that promise before. Patton did trust her. He didn't follow through with a residential program but instead banked on the fact that she would soon be busy again with sports since Emilie's recreational leagues for basketball and flag football were starting the next day. They would keep her active, integrated with her peers, and less bored, he assured me. I had no choice but to accept Patton's way of parenting even though I was the one responsible for monitoring and keeping her busy. My resentment built a little as I felt unheard but I accepted their agreement, praying she would stop.

I took Emilie to her first flag football practice the following day. She was excited as she walked on the field sporting her bright new pair of cleats. I was elated to see her rejuvenated enthusiasm for sports, and life.

The parking spot that I found was directly in front of where she and her teammates performed their drills. I watched from the comfort of my air-conditioned car. Emilie immediately showed dominance over the other players. She was not only the tallest on her team but appeared the fastest, strongest, and most well-prepared athlete as well.

Just ten minutes into a blocking drill, Emilie's eyebrow and her opponent's mouth collided. Ouch! I saw the opponent immediately place her hand up to her swollen lip and walk away into the rec center. Then I saw Emilie follow behind her and assumed that she was trying to comfort her. When they re-emerged about ten minutes later, Emilie looked distraught. I hurried from my car to see that she was hurt, too! I noticed right away the swelling and ¾-inch cut on her brow. I assumed it was from the impact of her eye glass frame and the force of the other player. Emilie was also pale and had perspiration droplets on her entire face. I told the coach I was not going to let her continue playing. When Emilie said that she didn't want to play anymore, I knew she must be hurting. It was rare for her to turn down playing nearly any sport!

After Emilie got into the car, I grew more concerned because of her profuse perspiration and sallow coloring. I didn't know much about concussions but I knew they

152

could be dangerous. I called Patton and asked him to meet us as I felt she needed to see a doctor right away.

At first, Patton told me to simply take her home and give her water and pain reliever. But I told him of her feeling dizzy and continuous cold sweat which didn't appear to be letting up, he agreed to meet me. At the nearby gas station where we met, Emilie moved into his car for him to drive her to the closest walk-in clinic. In route there, Emilie continued to show signs of a concussion and when she arrived at the clinic, they asked if she was having memory issues.

"Do you remember your name?"

"No."

"Do you know who this is?" The nurse asked while pointing to Patton.

"No."

The clinic administered oxygen and called for ambulatory services to take Emilie to the hospital. This was standard protocol for the clinic to do in the event of a concussion.

Patton called me at home and told me where they were going. I rushed to meet them in the emergency room.

When I walked in the room where Emilie lay in her gurney wearing nothing but her gown and a temporary neck brace, I fought the tears that welled in my eyes. I knew I had to stay strong but where was Patton? I walked up to Emilie and saw her with glassy eyes staring straight ahead. I talked to her and told her that I was there, in case she could understand me since she didn't appear to be fully lucid.

I prayed aloud to Jesus to watch over, protect, and heal her. I sobbed but gained my composure once again wondering where Patton was. I asked the staff and they indicated that he was out in the hallway. I quickly went to get him thinking that she needed her dad, not just me, to be by her side. Patton was on the phone informing his mother what had happened. I let him know I was there and quickly returned to Emilie's side.

I asked the doctor what I could do to help, if anything. He told me to just stay there and be by her side. I did.

I looked through my purse while trying to think of things to say or do to get a reaction from my stepdaughter to help bring her out of this trance-like state. I had never dealt with something like this, I was petrified. Did she have brain damage? Would she snap out of it? What was going on? The hit didn't appear to be that hard but clearly it was hard enough to put a gash over her eye. The incident did puncture the skin, yes, but not deep enough to create a need for stitches, so how could this be?

I remembered a funny song that she liked and tried to recall the words. It had profanity in it but I didn't care as I hoped that the mere fact I would sing something so silly might jar her a bit. Her eyes moved a bit and there was a slight reaction as if to say, "Hang it up, Lisa, don't sing that."

I reached into my purse finding nothing but my driver's license and another identification picture. I placed them in front of her eyes telling her how I looked ridiculous and may as well have shaved my head for the photo since my tight pony tail made it appear that way anyway.

She smiled!

A rush of comfort ran through me! I quickly got the words of the silly song back in my mouth and let them out softly, but purposefully. She half-laughed.

Ah, we were getting out of the woods!

I ran out to the hallway and retrieved Patton, telling him that Emilie was no longer non-reactive. I felt confident all would be well!

Patton and I hurried back to Emilie's bed and the doctors came to test her strength and feeling. She was still not squeezing the doctor's hand more than perhaps five percent of what she was capable but at least she was responding a bit. Then she was asked some basic yes or no questions to which she was able to respond. Thank

154

you, God! It took time, apparently to recover from a concussion but this was looking more promising at least.

About a half-hour later, Emilie was speaking quite clearly. She said she needed to use the restroom and I told her that a nurse would likely bring her a bed pan as I was pretty sure she wouldn't be allowed to just get up and go. She also needed a feminine sanitary product and I told her they would surely help her out with that as well.

She got a big smiling face on when she answered. "Yeah, that won't be happening. I can walk to a bathroom; I feel fine." I wasn't convinced although she was speaking quite clearly and appeared emotionally stable. I asked the doctor and he agreed that if a nurse could disconnect her IV fluid, and she felt able, she could go. I went out to the hallway to find a nurse.

They told us where the restroom was, and allowed me to walk with Emilie. Feeling uncomfortable in her gown and being naked underneath, she scurried toward the bathroom asking me to return to the emergency room to get her clothes while she waited. I ran back to the room and found her bag of cut clothing from the ambulance. Her shorts were okay but the rest were not. When I returned, she was happy to see that her shorts would cover her but disappointed that her favorite University of Florida Gator shirt was cut in half.

When we returned together, Emilie asked for her phone. She took a few selfie pictures and then posted them along with the details of her accident. She also texted a few people to tell them that she was in the hospital.

We were feeling hopeful about her discharge from the hospital but the E.R. doctor and a new doctor from the adjoining children's hospital said they wanted to keep her for observation overnight, just in case.

They led the way to the adjoining All Children's Hospital where Emilie would spend the night in a rather lovely suite. It was a colorful private room with a large flat-screen television, lots of video games and "room service"! Emilie would not hate this; no kid would! While she got situated in her bed, I gathered my purse and keys to go home to get Patton and her some personal items from our house.

I was only home for a few minutes after my fifteen-minute drive when Patton called to tell me that Emilie had begun slurring her speech and lost her memory. What?

When I arrived back in her hospital room I noticed that Emilie was now speaking in a childish sort of way. She wasn't enunciating and had a higher pitch than normal. She was speaking drawn-out words in baby talk. It was confusing but I knew nothing about concussions. I stayed for only a few more minutes and went home as only one parent could stay.

Wanting to know as much as I could about concussions, I went onto the Internet and started researching. I found that slurred speech was common initially and that often the incident causing the concussion would never be remembered. But Emilie had already recounted all the details on her social media post and had walked and talked perfectly, so I was confused but somewhat reassured. I also gleaned that concussions varied with different people depending on the severity.

Before I left for the hospital the next morning, Patton called to tell me that Emilie was doing the same as the night prior. She had no memory of many things and was still slurring her speech.

How could Emilie go from practically skipping to the bathroom, talking very normally (even joking) and recounting details of the incident in the emergency room to now behaving almost inebriated.

To add her symptoms, Emilie then announced that she couldn't walk! Although all of the initial x-rays, CAT scans and MRI's showed everything was normal, my stepdaughter couldn't move her legs. Was there something that might be overlooked? Was there a brain injury or neurological disorder from the concussion? She

156

spent a second night in the hospital for more observation and then was released.

When I spoke with my husband about what was wrong he said the doctors recommended further testing. He took her to a few different doctors who saw nothing physically to deter her mobility. I continuously read that concussions varied person to person. I had hoped Emilie wasn't "faking" anything and had no reason to believe she was, but I did suggest that maybe over the years with her mom as the primary influence in her life, perhaps she could have picked up the victim card? I wasn't at all sure and but I did suggest it as possibility. It wouldn't have been her fault had that been the case, it was her mother's, I implored. But Patton couldn't believe I would suggest such a theory. The last thread that held our severed relationship together, snapped.

The phone rang later the next evening. When I answered, Patton's mother told me she was driving down to help care for Emilie. I was taken aback. When I told my husband that I could handle it, she needn't drive so far, he laid into me. "No! I don't trust you with her! You don't believe her and you will try to make her walk! Then when she falls, she'll end up cracking her head open!"

Whoa! I had not expected that.

I was hurt since I was just as concerned if Emilie would ever get better or if this was permanent illness/disorder. *No one* seemed to know and Patton wasn't discussing anything with me any longer. I only learned about a few of their appointments from the random doctor bills and brochures he'd occasionally leave on the counter of our kitchen. Patton took her to a neurological center and for more tests. She had another CAT scan where the doctor did see that the initial CAT showed some brain swelling compared to the new one. There was no diagnosis, nor was there any indication of when she would resume clear speech or the ability to walk.

I was angry at myself for ever for a moment, doubting Emilie and her intentions but I was desperate for answers; we all were.

I wondered how her brain was working. Had the toll of lifelong mental and physical abuse from Andrea, watching her father be arrested, and the legal system depriving her of protection from her mother finally caught up to Emilie and manifested itself as some type of psychological or physiological disorder?

My earlier doubt apparently leaked to my husband's family and friends. I was instantly shunned.

Patton spent many sleepless nights wondering if his daughter's non-improving condition would be permanent. He was missing work for at least a few hours each day, if not the entire day, to watch over Emilie and take her to various specialists. Our bills were piling up with him not working steadily and his back began to get the best of him. He got Emilie a wheelchair so she could manage to get around on her own and he could return to work.

Just a few days after the wheelchair arrived, Emilie walked about five steps to the cable box on our built-in wall shelf. She had been sitting on the couch with Patton watching TV. Patton excitedly called out, "Honey!" As soon as she realized what she did, she said, "Oh wow!" and went jelly-legged.

She was capable of walking but she seemed to be psychologically blocking herself from doing so. I began to re-assess my feelings. I knew my stepdaughter, she was a *very* active girl. This had to be real or she *had* to at least be thinking this was real.

Days later, we were watching a movie which casted a little girl who was blind, only she wasn't; she could see perfectly fine. She had Conversion Disorder. I quickly left the room and researched this malady on the Internet.

On the Mayo Clinic Website it said:

"Conversion Disorder is a condition in which you show psychological stress in physical ways. The condition was so named to describe a health problem that starts as a

158

mental or emotional crisis — a scary or stressful incident of some kind — and converts to a physical problem. In conversion disorder, your leg may become paralyzed after you fall from a horse, even though you weren't physically injured. Conversion disorder signs and symptoms appear with no underlying *physical* cause, and you can't control them. Signs and symptoms of conversion disorder typically affect your movement or your senses, such as the ability to walk, swallow, see or hear. Conversion disorder symptoms can be severe, but for most people, they get better within a couple of weeks."[12]

This was it! It had to be!

Finally, some logical information! I felt so happy to find something that helped me to understand. It was psychological, not intentional at all. I excitedly took my computer and shared my findings with Emilie.

"I have heard that so many times from doctors but that is not what I have, Lisa! This is from my concussion!" She said angrily to me.

"But this, this makes sense! Don't you think so?" I tried enthusiastically.

"No, I have post-concussive disorder! I don't have something wrong with me mentally!" She said indignantly. I immediately thought how offensive this must have sounded to her. She didn't want the stigma of having something mentally "wrong" even though she didn't cause it.

"Okay, well you just said doctors have been saying this, and I didn't even know it existed but it does make sense. It isn't something you should be ashamed of; it is something that your brain is doing without your consent, honey." Gee, here I was trying to wash away the doubt I had and even given an apology but she wasn't having it even though (unbeknownst to me until that point) some doctors that Patton had taken her to, apparently suggested the same.

"No, I don't have that and I don't want to talk about it anymore!" She looked away.

When Patton got home, and I shared the information I just read. He told me that he showed me information about Conversion Disorder when they got back from the initial hospital stay. He told me that he had already told me about the doctors suggesting that it could be all or none of the reason that she wasn't walking. I told him he must have been confused with whom he told because it was definitely not me! We were rarely talking since he told me he "didn't trust me with [his] daughter". Had I known about this disorder, I would have been far more understanding and never had suggested any other reason. I felt so badly and begged for our family to mend, but it was too late. I was not being forgiven.

I asked Patton for a separation or divorce. He agreed. Our finances weren't prepared for my moving out just yet so we would be living together for at least another month after Christmas.

Patton and I celebrated Thanksgiving separately, each with our own families. My mother-in-law, who was staying with us intermittently rarely said a word to me or to McKenna before we left to go out of town. When we came back, we felt judged and unwelcomed so we went to stay at a friend's house on random nights or in the guest room of our own house. Patton and I were essentially roommates for the next two months.

When I awoke one morning a couple of weeks later I saw a "blade" on the kitchen counter. The blade was the same kind Emilie had cut with in the past. These were the from the security sensors tabs found in DVD cases. These tiny half-inch by 1 1/2" metal pieces were encased in plastic and adhered to the insides of movies and audio books. It had taken me hours to get rid of all of them from our 200 plus DVD collection, but here, two weeks later, I found one. After Emilie denied placing it there and Patton believing her, I felt internal anguish rising to the surface so retreated yet again with McKenna, to my friend's house.

I felt horrible moving my daughter back and forth during the week. We needed to reclaim our space; this was our home, too! Three days later, while still at my friend's house, I text-messaged Patton to see if he had the money necessary to assist my moving out. He said he did not, but we needed to talk about the terms.

I agreed to meet him the next day for breakfast.

Patton and I met at Cracker Barrel. When he arrived, he gave me a friendly hug and kissed my head. It was uncomfortable since I was thinking of our rendezvous as a business meeting of sorts.

At that point, I was a housewife for almost nine years with no recent work experience and no credit. I wasn't going to be greedy as Andrea was, I simply needed enough for a down payment of a house, $50k in a lump sum, and for him to pay my living expenses for twenty-four months while I got back on my feet.

While we both agreed to the financial terms, we also vowed that until McKenna and I moved out, we would be pleasant in front of the girls so not to upset either of them further.

It had now been close to a month since Emilie returned from the hospital and was wheelchair bound. Patton was out front putting Christmas lights on the bushes. Emilie sat in her wheelchair at the edge of the seawall out back, fishing. She looked so lonely, yet peaceful. I took the opportunity to go speak with my blondie. I hugged her lightly and told her that we were all under a lot of stress and sometimes things got the better of us. I reminded her of how our relationship with each other had blossomed so much over the last few years and that I loved her. We rarely had conflicts, I told her, because she was usually so mindful of me and that I was very appreciative of that. I told her how much happiness she brought into my life when we cooked together, played a game, or just laughed at silly videos.

She asked me to stay outside with her to watch her fish. That is how you knew that you were in good standing with Emilie; she invited you into her world. My skin covered in goose bumps and my eyes welled with tears of joy hidden behind my sunglasses.

With our pending move out time approaching, things remained a bit awkward at the house. However, we all managed to be civil to one another and less silent. I still loved my family I was just not feeling in love with my husband anymore.

Gradually over the next few days, we began acting once again, like roommates. I truly didn't mind since I had detached myself considerably from him. In contrast, my relationship with Emilie seemed to have resumed back to our happy place. I loved it, as peace was certainly a commodity those months.

Patton grew to trust me enough to stay with Emilie in her wheel chair and gradually began working full days again. Emilie and I kept busy those days while our relationship resumed positively. So much so in fact that when she said as she often did, "I hate being in this stupid wheel chair," I smiled enthusiastically and looked at her square in the eye. "You know, you could try to just use your mind and make yourself just get up right now, right this minute and do it! Just say 'I'm walking, I am done with this thing!'" You know how excited Daddy would be for you to walk to the door and open it for him when he got home from work?" I didn't want to pressure her but certainly tried to encourage her.

"What if I walked on Christmas Eve or woke up Christmas morning? He would be really happy!" She got caught up in the thought of such a surprise.

"Yes, that is for sure! Or you *could* do it now?" Why wait?" I cheered.

"I can't. My legs just hurt too much." She slumped in her chair.

"Okay, well, as I have been saying, your muscles have to be atrophying a bit by now, and I just know you want to be strong for all your sports. I just worry, the longer it takes, the less likely it may be that you'll get your full

162

strength back." A stepmom can try, but unfortunately, no luck.

Patton decided that for Christmas, he was going to take Emilie and her new dog to his mother's house on Christmas Eve. I had already purchased a few small gifts for my mother-in-law so I sent those with him even though she was no longer speaking to me. The gifts I got for Emilie and Patton were not yet wrapped so I told them they could open them when they returned.

The day after Christmas, I received a text from my husband with an attached video. It was a Christmas miracle! Emilie was walking! She was even running! She was out of that wheel chair! I teared up while I called Patton's cell phone. Emilie answered. Overwhelmed with joy, I told her how proud I was of her.

Patton later told me that she wasn't even jelly-legged. He told me he carried her down to the beach to watch her dog play in the water and as they sat on a towel together, he talked to her about overcoming her obstacles and how she had the power to do that. She had to have the will and desire to get past the many issues that stemmed from being raised by Andrea. After a minute or two, she stood up and walked down the beach with him. He said there was no fanfare, just a nice walk and talk with her.

When they arrived home a couple of days later, I was elated to see them both. Our marriage wouldn't be helped but the peace Patton and Emilie both had to feel from her being able to resume her physical independence would certainly benefit all of us in the house.

Just a week later, on New Year's Day, reality reared its ugly head again. Patton was going to the gym for an early afternoon workout. I mentioned I would be going also, but not for a half-hour or so. When Patton offered his daughter to accompany him, she said she would rather go with me. No problem, I was happy to have her go with me! Also, since her mother had made no attempt to contact her in the past three months or even send a response to the simple "Merry Christmas" email that

Emilie sent, I tried to show her the maternal love that she deserved and probably never felt from Andrea.

Just before the gym, Emilie asked me if we had any small pencil sharpeners. I told her yes, McKenna had a great electric one.

"Yes, but I want the tiny kind that I can put in my backpack for school." She answered.

"Oh, I don't know, go take a look around, check the pencil drawer." I had a sneaking suspicion what her motive was but I couldn't be sure.

"I already did but couldn't find any. Can we stop at Office Depot to get one?" She just confirmed my suspicion. School wasn't going to start for six days and at this point, she still wasn't allowed to go to her old school, nor was there a plan for a new school.

Oh no, here we go again, I thought.

"Well honey, it is New Year's Day. I am not even sure they are open today." They were, but I wanted to prevent her from cutting if that *was* her intention. She used only tiny blades and I guessed that begging for me to go get her a DVD would have been too suspect. Plus she knew the first thing I did with those was to remove the security sensor she so loved.

"I will call and see." Emilie offered; she was on a mission, like an addict. Not only did she call the closest Office Depot to see if they were opened, but I overheard her ask if they carried the "tiny little pencil sharpeners," that she wanted...needed. The first store referred her to another nearby store. She called that one then announced, "They have them at the thirty-fourth street location! But, they close at five. Can we stop there before the gym because they might be closed after we finish working out?" She begged me.

"Uh, okay, sure. But Emilie, school doesn't start for a week, do you really need that now?" I asked quizzically.

"I just want to be really prepared for school when it starts." Although she knew how intuitive I was all the time, she seemed to be unaware that I was onto her.

164

I quickly texted my husband about the sharpener mission.

Later that night when I emerged from the shower, I heard yelling going on between my husband and Emilie. They were in her room with the door shut. I checked on McKenna who was watching a movie at high volume in the guest room with a sleepover friend. .

Reassured about McKenna, I crouched down in the hall near Emilie's room to hear what was being said. Clearly, the pencil sharpener had opened Patton's eyes enough that he could see healing from the concussion and the Conversion Disorder didn't mean she was fully recovered internally.

Emilie was saying that she missed her sister, her cat and her things at her mother's house. She said she felt unloved and even hated. She said she had no friends and that her school was keeping her out, convincing the kids she was a crazy person with whom they should not befriend. This poor child felt excommunicated from society.

She continued. "Dad, you don't even believe me. I wanted to use the pencil sharpener to get prepared for school, not to cut! I don't want to go and get help at a residential facility! I want to be on some different medication. This Zoloft isn't working! Why can't they just put me on Prozac? That seems to help everyone else! You just don't understand everything that I am feeling. There is so much you don't know!" Crying profusely, she continued at high volume. He responded with sympathy but nothing consoled her.

When he finally walked out, I wasn't sure how things would go; she was exasperated, he was speechless. I tried to offer him a few words of comfort. "Patton, I am really sorry you have to go through all of this. I know it isn't easy." No response, not even a look in my direction. He was unpacking his gym bag in the bedroom we *used* to share.

165

Sulking, Emilie came in and plopped her upper body onto the end of my bed. She seemed to be looking for some reaction or words from my husband who was still bent over his gym bag.

I stood next to Emilie and lowered my hand onto her back, feeling her frustration from the warm perspiration that drenched her t-shirt. "Emilie, I am here for you if you ever just want to talk. I promise to just listen."

Emilie slid her body out of my reach. "I just want to be left alone. Dad will you please lift the dog on my bed?" Her bed in her room was a loft and she was strong but the dog was almost fifty pounds which made it difficult to lift her wiggling body over the bed frame.

I said goodnight to them and went to the guest room to say the same to McKenna and her overnight guest then I left to sleep in McKenna's empty room. Patton came in a few moments later. He had Emilie's phone in his hand.

"How do I look up her search history?" He asked me quietly. I smiled and showed him. It was rare for him to take my advice but I was glad this was one of those times. I had suggested several times in the past that he look at her search history as a way of understanding her better.

He found many searches about the blades from pencil sharpeners along with other inquiries using the terms "girl with abs", "vomiting", "cutters self-harm", and "tongue screen diet", whatever that was? He didn't say a word just returned to our bedroom where Emilie was waiting.

Emilie was upset with me for not keeping the sharpener a secret and it now seemed that Patton was mad at me again, too?

After several days of virtual silence between us, while doing the laundry in the laundry room that is on the other side of Emilie's wall, I overheard Emilie talking about things that should have triggered a phone call for help by Patton. But, instead he just listened.

"You just don't understand, dad, I hate my life! You spend all this money to get custody; now you have me and

I hate my life!" She went on from there without Patton interrupting.

"I hate my life; it is so boring. I wake up every day, stretch, have a smoothie, do my virtual school thing, watch TV, and wait a few hours for you to come home. Then we go work out, and maybe do something. We eat, maybe fish until dark, or something, and then watch TV again until it is time to go asleep. It is so boring."

"Well honey, I know a lot of kids would kill to have every day be like that." Patton retorted.

Although I didn't care for Patton's choice of verbs, it was exactly what I was thinking behind the wall.

"I just want to get out of this house. I just feel like I miss the things at my mom's house. I miss my iPad, and my skateboard, even though they're from the Salvation Army. I miss my cat; I miss my sister. I just miss my things. I mean I was an abused kid and now I'm not, but I don't have my school. I don't have my friends. I just don't have anything." I could hear the loneliness in Emilie's voice. The kids had just returned from Christmas break so it didn't help reading about her peers on social media updates.

"I'm so sorry honey." Patton said sympathetically.

I returned to my room to go to bed. Emilie was feeling like a victim just as her mom had always done. The difference was, Emilie *deserved* to feel this way because she *was* a true victim. I simply couldn't hear the pain anymore without resenting Patton for not taking her to an inpatient treatment facility. His reason was two-fold: he didn't want to send her somewhere unless she agreed that she wanted and needed the help, and the cost was extremely prohibitive. Although Andrea was the abuser who ultimately created this condition in my stepdaughter, she wouldn't pay a penny toward any of her recovery or treatment just as she never contributed to *any* of Emilie's expenses.

Patton wasn't comfortable leaving Emilie alone as he was still concerned she could be suicidal. He needed to come up with the money for treatment as he could never be at peace with his worries until she was under the care of professionals equipped to handle her issues.

Early the next day, Emilie asked me where the pencil sharpener was. This was a full week after we bought that infamous little tool. When I told her that I didn't know, her dad had it, she just walked away. I texted Patton as a courtesy to let him know. I wasn't sure if he was preoccupied, angry, focused or why he was aloof with me, but I needed to be away from him so not to feel so ignored and perhaps not be a part of Emilie's problem.

Our separation could not come soon enough.

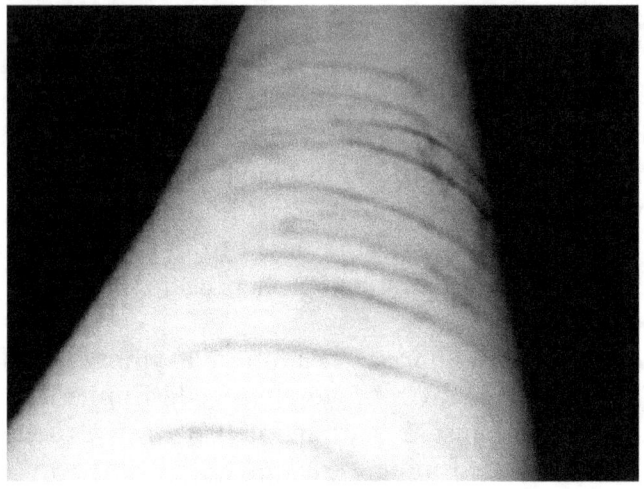

This is not Emilie. Her cutting was far more severe and all over her body.

XIX: Separate Lives

I didn't choose a Bible verse for this chapter as I have to really think about what role God played at this juncture; He seemed to play a lot of roles.

On February 1, 2014, I took McKenna and myself away from the decade of drama that began with Patton's ex-wife and manifested itself like a terminal cancer in his daughter, my marriage, and our family as a whole. I needed out. McKenna and I moved into a condominium rental with a one-year lease. I had no job history since we married and needed to build credit before I could buy another home. While I resented certain aspects of my marriage, my departure wasn't ugly; it was accepting and mature, probably because we still loved each other.

Patton and I agreed to the financial terms and I didn't want either of us to have to pay attorneys as he was struggling so much from custody and alimony payments to Andrea in the past, investments, his custody litigation and now Emilie's therapy, attorneys, Guardian Ad Litem, too many doctors to count, and special private schools for Emilie. Patton continued to provide a good lifestyle for his daughter, and for two years provided fairly for McKenna and me, as I got back on my feet. I have no animosity for Patton, just sympathy and abiding love for him.

Since I moved out, Patton and I actually began dating again and talking on a regular basis. He apologized profusely about all I had been through with him and his lack of consideration for my feelings. While I believed him, I knew we at least needed a one-year separation before we determined what was best.

In February and early March, we talked about Emilie's continuous cutting and the dark comments she typed on her social media accounts. Emilie also had bouts of eating issues soon after McKenna and I moved out and her lying was perpetuating. She was cutting again. Patton would take Emilie to his office which is in a high-rise downtown

St. Petersburg. There were restrooms on each floor. Apparently, Emilie had been cutting there and even posted a photo with her bloody forearm while she was in one of those restrooms. She wasn't being helped and Patton needed to find a way to make it happen, financially.

Emilie's sad life, I believe can be attributed to the injustice from our legal system. The pain her mother caused certainly initiated her plight as a child but the legal system had several chances to stop it, they didn't. They instead facilitated and empowered Andrea to physically and emotionally harm her daughter for the duration of her childhood. Andrea and the judges who neglected to help this innocent child, should have been responsible for a treatment program for Emilie, but they weren't. Patton was the only one who cared about his daughter's well-being and treatment. He just wanted his daughter to have a normal life.

Even though Emilie was seeing a counselor on a regular basis, she was Baker Acted yet again (for the fourth time) about six weeks after McKenna and I moved out. She impeded Patton's ability to work a proper week, taking away his ability to support himself and his family without difficulty. He was constantly preoccupied and emotionally tormented because he was worried about Emilie twenty-four hours a day. He was sleep deprived and often awoke in the middle of the night due to his anxiety. He was the most genuinely caring and devoted father that I had ever known, just as I witnessed the moment I met him.

Patton found a program called Teen Challenge at the Alabama/Georgia state line. It was an all-girls Christian based therapeutic residential facility that he was comfortable with. Emilie was ready and Patton somehow managed to pay the $3500 monthly tuition for the next seventeen months. Before he left to take her there in April 2014, I asked if he and Emilie would like to come over to my place for her favorite home-cooked meal. They agreed. The dinner went well but the goodbye was bittersweet. I took comfort knowing that my stepdaughter's healing was finally about to commence.

A few days later, Patton feeling somewhat relieved that his daughter was now in good hands at a safe Christian environment, had a little more time to focus on other aspects of his own life. While we were on a dinner date one evening, he reiterated that my absence had been an eye opener to him. He finally acknowledged that I was a valuable part of our home, family, marriage, and his happiness. He said he would spend the rest of his life making it up to me. Although my heart was touched, I was blanketed in peace now and still carried resentment. I was treated so unfairly when I questioned the validity of Emilie's inability to walk. More importantly, my not being able to act as a true parent and not respected as an equal during our marriage had pushed me to my limit. I wasn't ready to make a permanent decision to divorce or stay separated so we did the latter for the next year and half while continuing to date and try counseling.

While Emilie resided in the Teen Challenge program, strict guidelines were enforced about whom and how often she was able to communicate. For the first couple of months, there was no communication allowed but the program did give weekly updates by phone to the parents. Interestingly enough, although Andrea and Emilie never once spoke, even by email since the order in September 2013, Andrea suddenly contacted the boarding school. After the initial contact waiting period, each child was allowed twenty-minutes of phone time with parents only. Patton had already shared the details of the no-contact order against Andrea but the school administrators felt it would be counter-productive for Emilie to not be able to speak with her for at least half of her allotted time each month. So Emilie did.

After speaking with Andrea the first time, Emilie expressed great concern over what her mother was saying to her. Andrea knew the call was supervised when she said that she had been trying to see Emilie but her father wouldn't let her. Andrea hadn't changed, lies were still her main vice. The next call, Andrea tried to sound concerned about her daughter. This confused my stepdaughter.

Months into the program, parents (only) were finally permitted to visit for a few hours. You would have thought my husband won the lottery; he couldn't have been more excited to see her! Both Patton and Andrea showed up for the visit yet neither spoke with the other. Patton had always played fair and although Emilie joyfully cried at the sight of her dad and stayed by his side, Patton still had hope for Andrea and Emilie to reconcile. He prayed that his ex-wife would acknowledge and finally apologize for what she had done to their daughter. He urged Emilie to go speak with her mother. "Honey, your mom came all the way up here, she is over there by herself, why don't you take the first few hours with her and then I will spend the rest of your time with you."

After Emilie spent an hour or so with her mother, she went to speak with her father and one of her counselors. Emilie said she was very scared and worried. She said that her mother still denied ever doing anything wrong and that she called her a liar. Her mother told her that she was filing for custody and going to get her out of there. Emilie told Andrea she didn't want to live with her, that she wanted to live with her dad when she was finished with the program. Further, Andrea was lying, she hadn't filed for restored custody and even downsized her home and moved into a two bedroom place for only herself and Sarah. All the while also telling little Sarah that her big sister was "bad."

Emilie's stress level appeared to have returned to the state it was when she was first Baker Acted. She cut herself again while at the school just after seeing and speaking with her mother. Patton attributed it to Emilie's fear of her mom coming to take her. Patton refused to have his daughter's progress jeopardized. He immediately filed a motion with the courts to have ALL of Andrea's contact rights removed.

On August 4, 2014, I received a call on my cell phone from a number marked "private". I couldn't believe it! It was Andrea!

She started talking all sweetly saying how she wished she had gotten the chance to really talk to me during many of the times there was trouble with Emilie. I was so astounded by her attempt I just played along with brief answers at first.

"...Lisa, there is so much that you don't know, you have no idea. These lies from Emilie and Patton. I was just hoping you and I could meet somewhere and talk." Was she crazy? I would never trust this woman. Obviously, she must have been privy to the fact that Patton and I had separated. But she didn't know the whole story.

"Andrea, I agree that there is plenty I probably don't know..." I tried to respond but she couldn't help herself from speaking over me.

"No, I mean you realize there are some serious issues going on with that family (referring to my in-laws). I mean Patton's father used to beat and abuse him and then his sister well, she was an alcoholic and died of that!" I guess she thought she could talk about my husband's family and I would jump on board to become an ally. Yes, his sister did die from alcoholism about a decade prior but no, his father did not abuse, nor beat, my husband! He was a pastor and a good and decent man who passed away before Andrea's physical abuse was exposed, his son was arrested, and Emilie's cutting began. I resented her speaking that way about my father-in-law so I immediately got in defense mode.

"Andrea, you must be aware that Patton and I are no longer living together but what you may not be aware of is that we still love each other and see each other. Patton's father never abused him, how dare you say that and if I were you, I would go get some counseling to become the best mother you can be to Emilie." I tried to remain calm but my voice trembled from the confrontation.

She began to reply, "Well you ..." as soon as I heard her tone, I knew I must hang up on her, so I did.

I shared her call with Patton and the conversation that took place. I asked him if he wanted me to come to the hearing (to abolish Andrea's contact altogether with Emilie) that upcoming Wednesday to support him. He did.

When Andrea saw me accompanying my husband to the hearing, she looked livid. My body reacted the way it usually did, shaky and nervous, but I wouldn't let her know it. I smiled contently as I thought of her phone call. She actually thought after all she had done to her daughter and all the attempts she made to destroy my family, she may have somewhat succeeded in breaking our unity but she was wrong. I was there with Patton, for Emilie, against her.

Patton and I were even more gratified as the hearing was surprisingly successful! It was Judge D (yes, another new judge) who stripped Andrea's right to communicate with Emilie while she was away and also ordered that neither parent be able to remove the child from the school unless they got the court's approval.

Andrea was no longer winning all the time and that did not suit her well. We knew how she would take her frustration and temper out on Emilie so we couldn't help but worry about Sarah. George was concurrently filing motions against Andrea. He wanted to have a Guardian appointed for his daughter, for Andrea to be ordered for psychological testing, and for her visitation rights removed. Sarah had expressed numerous times that she was experiencing her mother's yelling and finger poking. He knew it would only get worse given what Andrea had done to Emilie. Per George, Sarah cried every time he had to take her back to her mother. The judge granted the motion for the Guardian to be appointed and future hearings for the other motions. Thankfully, the GAL was the same one appointed to Emilie so she was already familiar with Andrea.

Emilie persevered at her school where she had good days and bad. She eventually became comforted upon learning that her mother could no longer visit, write, or call her directly and felt better that Sarah now had Irene in her corner. Emilie and I kept in touch through the mail a few times and my faith grew stronger that she would have healing from her lifetime of abuse she suffered at the hands of Andrea. I told Emilie in one of my letters that no matter what happened between her dad and me, I would be there for her if ever she needed a maternal figure in her life. I meant it from my heart. I even cried while writing it, thinking of how close we had become over the years. This child, any child, should never feel abandoned and I loved my stepdaughter.

Patton and I continued dating while Emilie was in the program. Although I was still hopeful to reconciling our marriage, I was wary about Andrea and the battle that wouldn't truly be over until Emilie was eighteen. I appreciated his intent to "spend the rest of [his] life making it up" to me, but he needed to be there for his daughter first and foremost, particularly since he lost a year and a half with her. He ultimately let it be my decision to divorce or not. Although I vacillated back and forth, I knew Patton needed an unbiased witness if he was going to keep Andrea legally from interfering with Emilie's progress. My being married to him would be too prejudicial. We officially divorced in July, 2015.

That same month, Andrea created a YouTube® video which she also shared on her Facebook® account, and on GoFundMe.com. For over five minutes, a very emaciated and seemingly desperate looking Andrea, spoke about being "a survivor of domestic violence" from Patton. Andrea was vain and would never let people know that *she* was the one who was diagnosed with NPD, had in-home child abuse counseling, as well as losing her rights to see or to communicate with her daughter. Andrea said Emilie began cutting because she "missed her mother so much," which of course wasn't true. Emilie began cutting *at* her mother's house during the forty-two days when she was kept her from her father. She was also first Baker Acted while in her *mother's* care. Andrea said she didn't have the money for an attorney to fight Patton anymore. She attempted to cry but never managed any tears. Her frequent and random eye movement was certainly indicative of her deceit but apparently she hoodwinked a few people since she raised over $1000 and dozens of people were "sharing" her video. Andrea was delusional and getting away with blatant slander. Patton was never arrested for domestic violence, he was arrested for "interference with custody," and the butt-dial from her fictitious court-shopping restraining order that never should have been granted temporarily. Although Patton, his attorney, and myself all contacted GoFundMe.com to remove the video, they declined, as did the police. They said if Andrea believed that she and her daughters were victims of domestic violence, then she wasn't committing slander. This was ridiculous.

Andrea, a year after she told Emilie she did while at Teen Challenge, began filing pro se for custodial time with Emilie. She filed nonsense self-serving journals, photos, emails, Patton's mugshot, and a litany of other seemingly disparaging exhibits against Patton.

Just before Emilie was due to graduate from her 17-month program, Andrea's requested hearing was before yet another new judge. Judge E was a female who could have passed for a relative of Emilie's with her blond hair and natural, all-American-girl look. Patton expressed that Andrea's presence or communication with Emilie once she came home to St. Petersburg, would take her right back to that dark place where she felt unprotected and unsafe from her mother. Her Honor agreed. She denied Andrea's request and told Andrea she was not to attempt *any* communication by phone, writing or appearance, including the new high school she would be attending, and any sport practices, games, etc.

Emilie graduated a few weeks later in mid-August, 2015.

I was happy to help prepare the welcome home party at Patton's house while he went to get her. It was a very joyous day with Sarah, George, his significant other Mary, Andrea's parents, the Guardian Ad Litem, and some family friends. Emilie looked great and seemed so content. It was the happiest I remembered seeing her since she first came to stay with us those two weeks after the discovery of her abuse (before the cutting, the arrests, and the seven-week custody withholding from Andrea).

Emilie was devout to the Lord and vowed to honor and worship Him. She would never cut or self-harm again. We believe her so long as she didn't see or hear from Andrea.

Unfortunately, since Emilie has been back, she has been on the cusp of developing an eating disorder.

While this is where my story ends, to date, there is still a lifetime journey of healing ahead for Emilie and will be the same for the countless victims of parental alienation.

I urge readers to share this story and contact their legislators about formally including the term "parental alienation" as a form of "Child Abuse." The laws must change to save these innocent children. We must also reform our family law to allow equal time-sharing for both parents unless there is evidence that it would not be in the best interest of the child. Without this, there is little hope to stop this cruel behavior.

(Left) Patton & Emilie at Church 2006.

(Right)Our family at Patton's brother's wedding in Boston 2008.

(Left) Emilie in her social media post when the judge wouldn't grant her an injunction against her mother.

Me, proud stepmom of a healing Emilie after coming home from Columbus Academy for Girls 2015.

Acknowledgements

To McKenna, my mother, father, and sister, I thank you for your patience, compassion, and unconditional support while listening to, advising, and encouraging me over the years and especially while I penned this narrative.

To Patton, I know we will always have regrets and apologies but I believe we will always have a respect and love for each other knowing that we survived so much turbulence. My heart will always belong to you and our daughters.

To my stepdaughter, Emilie, I thank you for allowing me the privilege of being a stepmom to you and trusting me to speak up regarding your deserved innocence. I know that your life was not what it should have been. I apologize for any angst I may have contributed and hope this book helps you and others like you. I wish you a very blessed and peaceful future filled with love.

To my dear friend, Lisa R., you have not only listened through my frustration and sometimes tears, but as a rare female victim of parental alienation by your own former spouse, your empathy helped fuel my passion to share this story in hopes of effecting a change for all parents and more so, for the children parental alienation.

Bibliography

[1] "Parental Alienation Syndrome." *Parental Alienation Crisis.* July 2012 <http://www.parentalalienationcrisis.org/index.asp?pageid=65505>

[2] Gardner, Richard. "Custody Disputes Fueling 'Parental Alienation Syndrome.'" *FAMILY PRACTICE NEWS.* Volume 20, Number 24, December 15-31, 1990, p7. September 2012 <http://www.fact.on.ca/Info/pas/gardnr90.htm>

[3] Hare, Robert. Without Conscience. New York: Guilford, 1993

[4] Hare, Robert. Without Conscience. New York: Guilford, 1993

[5] "Guidelines for Child Custody Evaluations in Family Law Proceedings" *APA.* American Psychologist Association. Dec 2010 Vol. 65 No. 9, 863-867. July 2012 <http://www.apa.org/practice/guidelines/child-custody.pdf p.864>

[6] Koller, Terrence. "Should There Be Immunity for Custody Evaluators?" *APA Divisions.* Wash, DC Aug. 2005. APA. Jun 2012 <http://www.apadivisions.org/division31/publications/articles/resources/immunity-custody.pdf>

[7] "The 2012 Florida Statutes." *Online Sunshine.* Oct. 2012 <http://www.leg.state.fl.us/statutes/index.cfm?App_mode=Display_Statute&Search_String=&URL=0000-0099/0061/Sections/0061.08.html>

[8] Online Sunshine. http://www.leg.state.fl.us/Statutes/index.cfm?App_mode=Display_Statute&URL=0800-0899/0827/Sections/0827.03.html

[9] "Judicial Case Management Practices Vary Throughout the State; Better Case Data Needed." *EDocs State of Florida.* Oppaga. Jan. 2009 Rep. No. 09-06. Aug. 2012 <http://edocs.dlis.state.fl.us/fldocs/leg/oppaga/2009/0906rpt.pdf>

[10] Online Sunshine. http://www.leg.state.fl.us/Statutes/index.cfm?App_mode=Display_Statute&URL=0800-0899/0827/Sections/0787.03.html

[11] Baker Act-Florida Department of Children and Families. http://www.dcf.state.fl.us/programs/samh/mentalhealth/docs/Baker%20Act%20Overview%202013.pdf

[12] Mayo Clinic website. http://www.mayoclinic.com/health/conversion-disorder/DS00877